THE

SUCCESSFUL SALES ASSISTANT'S HANDBOOK

New York Institute of Finance

Library of Congress Cataloging-in-Publication Data

The successful sales assistant handbook.

   Includes index.
   1. Securities—Handbooks, manuals, etc.   2. Brokers—
Handbooks, manuals, etc.   I. New York Institute of
Finance.   II. Title: Sales assistant handbook.
HG4621.S84   1987   332.6'2'0688   87-11322
ISBN 0–13–860305–7

This publication is designed to provide accurate and authoritative information in regard to the subject matter covered. It is sold with the understanding that the publisher is not engaged in rendering legal, accounting, or other professional service. If legal advice or other expert assistance is required, the services of a competent professional person should be sought.

From A Declaration of Principles Jointly Adopted by a Committee of the American Bar Association and a Committee of Publishers and Associations

New York Institute of Finance
(NYIF Corp.)
70 Pine Street
New York, New York 10270

How to Use This Manual

No one can write a procedures manual to meet your individual needs or your firm's requirements. No one, that is, but you.

This manual enables you to create—easily and step-by-step—your own procedures and reference manual. Each section provides the information you need to know, or asks the questions you need to answer, in order to be a more efficient, more effective, and less harried sales assistant. By the time you have followed the instructions in this book, you will have a brief handbook containing *your* personalized notes and *your firm's* forms and procedures.

While putting together your own procedures and reference manual, you will have the help of "experts," that is, the account executive, the operations manager, the cashier, and other key employees in your company. These people are "experts" because they know the firm's requirements and policies, and you can tap into their know-how.

When you are done, you will have a looseleaf binder that contains, in one place, all the forms, memos on procedure, and *any* other documents that you need to have readily on hand to do your job.

The first step is easy. This book has three punched holes and perforations running down the inside margin of the page. The perforations are there because the first thing you should do with this manual is tear out—carefully—all the pages along the perforations and place them into a looseleaf binder. (Your firm probably has binders with the company name and logo on them.) Use a 2- or 3-inch binder, since you'll be adding things to it even after completing this manual.

Once you have your binder set up, turn to the first page of Section 1—and take the second step toward becoming a successful sales assistant.

Contents

Contents

Your Position As Sales Assistant

The securities industry is fast paced, intense and ever-changing. Each business day, thousands of transactions are completed, many within a matter of seconds.

These transactions are the lifeblood of your employer's business because they generate the commission business your firm needs to operate profitably. As a result, transactions must be handled accurately and efficiently if your branch is to succeed. And this is where you come in as an essential member of the team.

As a sales assistant you help registered representatives by answering client questions about their accounts, verifying the accuracy of trades, and insuring that new accounts or account changes are processed promptly. (By the way, registered representatives are also called account executives, or financial consultants. The most popular name, however, is "broker.")

What do you think would happen to your firm's profits if you were discourteous to clients, handled trades carelessly, or took care of account changes at your leisure? The answer is clear and emphasizes the critical importance of the sales assistant role in operations.

The Branch Structure and Where You Fit In

Some large firms maintain hundreds of branch offices; a small firm may have only one. The office may be staffed by dozens of sales personnel, or have only one sales person. It may offer many different investment products and services, or it may specialize in a single type of investment—bonds, for example. but, whatever the incidental differences, the following key functions are common to all branches. Some branches are organized as shown in Figure 1-1. This chart represents a *clinical* view of the branch office and the functions it performs to service the clients of the firm. Depending on its location, size, volume, or number of clients, there may be additional job titles. For example, there may be a sales manager or administrative manager in addition to the operations manager. In this case, the branch office could be organized as shown in Figure 1-2.

Depending on the work load, some branch offices may have two people performing the same function, such as two operations managers or two cashiers. In other offices, one person may perform the functions handled by two or more people at a larger branch. For example, the credit clerk will not be a separate function. Instead, the operations manager will perform the necessary credit work. Such a branch may look like Figure 1-3.

The branch manager is generally allowed considerable freedom to organize the office in a way that is most conducive to doing business efficiently. This manager is ultimately responsible and accountable for every person and each task in that branch. Therefore, there are many different ways your branch can be organized. The three presented here are merely typical examples.

Notice, though, that in all three structures, a dotted line links the sales assistants with the account executives. This is because the work performed by the sales assistants directly assists the account executives and their clients. However, because the sales assistants are employed by the brokerage firm, the branch manager is responsible for their assignments.

Figure 1-1.

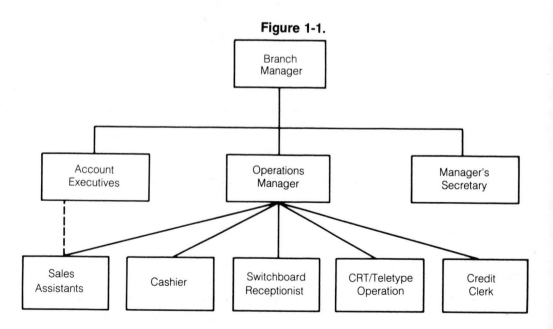

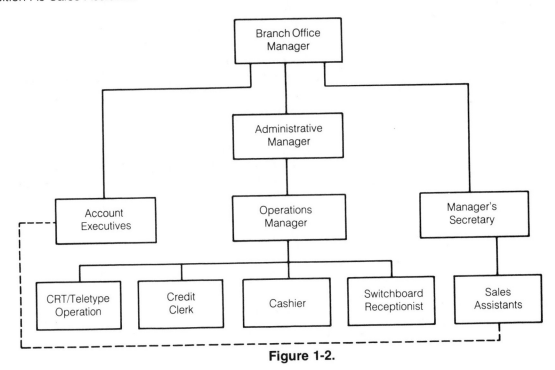

Figure 1-2.

Although the administrative structure of offices may vary, branch offices have one thing in common: they depend on the investment activity generated by the brokers and paid for by the clients for their survival.

One last note: Throughout this text, we speak of the sales assistant and the registered representative, or broker, as though it were a one-to-one work relationship. In practice, the sales assistant will work for two or more brokers.

Figure 1-3.

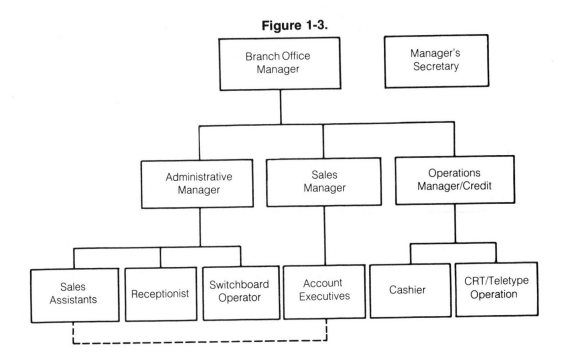

Branch Roles Defined

The Branch Manager

The branch manager is "captain of the ship." Everything that occurs within the branch office is the manager's ultimate responsibility. The branch manager's responsibilities include:

- Checking with the account executive on a regular basis to make certain that investments—both those suggested and those actually purchased—are in accordance with each client's objectives.

- Responding to any complaints made by clients or providing general service to them.

- Keeping a daily log of all business conversations with clients and account executives.

- Allocating new issues among the account executives for them to offer to their clients.

- If options are traded in the branch, making certain that all options accounts are operating within the guidelines set by the exchanges and the Options Clearing Corporation (OCC).

- If commodity futures are traded in the branch, making certain that the registered representatives who conduct futures business are approved by the futures exchanges and that the accounts are operating within the guidelines of those exchanges' rules and regulations.

- Managing the personnel of the office, including hiring and firing.

- Assisting in the training of account executives.

- Motivating account executives by assisting in the development and execution of sales ideas.

- *Perhaps most important,* insuring that the accounts, the branch, and its personnel are all operating within the procedures and budgetary constraints established by the firm.

Some of these responsibilities may be delegated to the sales, administrative, or operations managers. However, the ultimate responsibility is the branch manager's.

The Branch Operations (Office) Manager

The branch's operations manager (often abbreviated as BOM) oversees the operational support provided in the office. This includes making sure that the operations areas are properly staffed, providing account executives with adequate support, resolving operational problems, supervising the employees in the branch who are responsible for these operational functions, and insuring that account executives and their accounts are in compliance with the various rules and regulations of the regulatory agencies and the firm. In this way the operations manager plays a crucial role in servicing client accounts and protecting the firm's assets.

In many firms, small offices are branches of a parent branch. In this case, the operations manager may be physically located in the parent branch. The function is always available at the parent branch.

The Account Executive

Every account maintained by a firm is placed in the care of an individual known as an account executive. These individuals must be approved by several regulatory agencies before they are permitted to oversee accounts—even their own. New account executives, known as trainees, are chosen by the firm's management from among many highly qualified candidates. Experienced account executives may also join a firm after having first worked at another brokerage firm.

The newly-registered account executives set out to develop their own list of clients, whose investment accounts they will maintain. Each time a transaction is made in a client's account, the account executive earns a percentage of the commission the firm charges for executing the trade. These commissions provide the account executive's income and are the most important source of revenue to the brokerage firm.

It is the account executive who calls potential clients, popularly called *prospects*. Prospects may be obtained from the membership list of a local professional organization or a group of names suggested by a current client. The broker tries to interest the individual in the firm's investment services, to find out what the person's investment needs are, and to obtain an order. The account executive has then succeeded in opening a new account. He or she will continually make recommendations to the client for additional investments and will contact as many other potential new clients as possible. Each new account and every transaction made in those accounts are entered in the account executive's *book*.

It is important for the sales assistant to remember that the book is the property of the member firm. It may never be removed from the office. And, it should not be copied or otherwise tampered with. In effect, the book is a working legal document.

The typical account executive or registered representative book is divided into two parts. The first part is a listing by client; the second by securities held. Each time the account executive's clients purchase or sell securities through the firm, the transactions are noted in both sections. Maintenance of this book is required by law and is important because it gives the account executive an up-to-the-minute picture of each account under his or her jurisdiction as well as total security positions by client account.

The new *account* page plays a key role in the client/account executive relationship. This page gives the history as well as the current status of the client's account. It is a quick reference to when and at what price securities were bought or sold.

The *security* page informs the account executive of the securities owned by his or her clients and which clients they are. Therefore, when news breaks on a particular issue, the account executive opens the book to that security page and begins to call those clients listed on this page who have involvement in this security.

The Role of the Sales Assistant

The sales assistant helps account executives perform some of their functions. What sales assistants do varies from firm to firm and even within firms, but important responsibilities affecting all is *the answering of client questions about their accounts, verifying the accuracy of trades, and insuring that new accounts or account changes are processed promptly.*

The importance of courteous and accurate responses to client's questions cannot be overemphasized. Your firm spends a small fortune on advertisements to attract clients; the account executives spend hours on the telephone soliciting new accounts and explaining new investments to both new and current clients. All this can be lost or wasted if a sales assistant is curt or gives bad information.

Verifying the accuracy of trades accomplishes three goals:

1. It assures that the proper amount has been billed for the trade.

2. It confirms that the right security was in fact traded.

3. And, when a trade is posted in the book, the process helps to discover erroneous transactions.

You should note that some firms or branch managers permit only the account executives to post their books because they consider posting to be of critical importance in giving account executives control of their accounts. Still, it is useful to the sales assistant to review the posting of books to see the type of information provided and to become familiar with the client's business in order to service the account effectively and speak intelligently with the client.

Satisfied clients very seldom take their business elsewhere—although they may have a second account at another firm. Comparing the trade confirmation and the original order is a personal service that helps to keep the client satisfied. To make certain that the trade was processed for the right client, the sales assistant compares the account number on the confirmation with the number on the order ticket, thus assisting in the verification process.

When the sales assistant discovers that a trade was in fact processed to the wrong account, the client who will receive the erroneous confirmation should be called immediately. The phone call alerts the client to the error and offers assurances that the account is being conscientiously maintained. And don't forget, an error in one account is often an error in a second. Thus, a correct confirmation can be prepared and mailed to the right client before there is any sign that something went wrong.

Confirming that the right security was traded serves the client and protects the firm. When the trade is made, the firm enters into a binding contract. Suppose, for example, the client has ordered 100 shares of XYZ Corp., but 100 shares of XVZ Corp. had been purchased instead. To correct the error, the firm must sell the XVZ stock and buy the XYZ as requested. If the price of XYZ stock rises or that of XVZ falls between the time the original order is executed and the error found and corrected, the firm will have to absorb the loss. The sooner the error is detected, the greater the protection to the firm. Always be on the lookout for errors. The sales assistant helps protect the firm as well as serve the client.

The sales assistant also assists the new account processor when new accounts are opened as well as when they must be updated. The new account form must be completed at the branch level and signed by the registered representative and the branch manager. Other forms *must* be completed by the client.

The role of the sales assistant is to expedite this paper flow so that the firm's regulatory responsibility is satisfied as quickly as possible and that the accounts are opened and maintained properly.

In addition to the account executive and sales assistant, the branch office is made up of several operations and administrative personnel.

Branch operations include the following three functions:

- Cashier;
- CRT Operator (Communications);
- New Accounts Processor.

The number of employees needed to perform each of these functions depends on the size of the branch office.

The Branch Cashier

The branch cashier receives securities, cash, and checks from the clients. These items are "received in" to the clients' accounts with the help of *stock received* or *cash received* forms. At the end of each day, the securities are forwarded to the main office, and cash and checks are deposited at the branch's bank. The cashier then prepares *stock received* and *cash received* forms for the CRT operator, who transmits the information to the main cashier's department in the home office. This process is often called Stock Over the Wire (SOW) and Cash Over the Wire (COW).

The cashier also prepares checks for clients. When a client wishes to withdraw funds, the account executive (or sales assistant with account executive approval) prepares a check request which is forwarded to the cashier. The cashier, after verifying that there is sufficient cash in the client's account, draws the check and debits the client's account.

Margin Function (Sometimes Performed In Branch —Sometimes In Main Office)

The margin function includes preparation of the *item due list.* This list, which may have different names but always has the same function, is distributed to the account executives and tells them who among their clients owes either funds or securities. It then becomes the responsibility of the account executive or sales assistant to secure the needed item. Customer accounts must be maintained under the rules of the Federal Reserve, known as Regulation T, and those of the Self-Regulatory Organizations (SRO). The N.Y.S.E. rules and the NASD rules are examples of such regulations.

A customer failing to meet these established requirements is not living up to the terms of the account agreement and may also be in violation of an SRO rule or Regulation T. When this occurs, action must be taken in the account to correct the violation. If the violations are severe enough, the firm's compliance department may order the account closed. To avoid unnecessary problems, and to prevent minor problems from growing into serious ones, the sales assistant should cooperate closely with the margin employee in the branch to resolve all such problems daily.

The margin function will also give account executives the information they need before they buy or sell securities in a client's account. The margin person could be asked, "If account 0013456 sold 100 POP @ 36, how much buying power would it then have?" In other words, with the $3,600 (less commissions) from the sale of POP, plus the cash already in the account, how much more stock could be bought for account 0013456? Or, "How much margin would be necessary to support the sale of 10 RAM Oct 50 calls?" Since these questions are about trading stocks or options, the margin person will know what the margin requirements are. The margin person constantly answers such "what if" questions like these about accounts.

The CRT Operator

Orders received by the CRT operator from the account executives are entered into the firm's communication network. Here they are routed to the point of execution. This can be either one of the exchanges or the firm's over-the-counter department. When the orders are executed, these locations will notify the branch as well as the firm's operations area.

New Accounts Function

The new accounts function allows the sales assistant to assist the new accounts processor in securing the forms needed to open a new account and to obtain a new account number. The account may be an individual account, a partnership account, a joint account, or a trust. It may also be a corporation's account. It may have limited or full power of attorney, or it may combine two or more types. Some accounts permit margin transactions, others do not.

The new accounts processor is responsible for assembling the necessary forms, handing them to the client or giving them to the sales assistant to give or mail to the client. The new accounts processor is responsible for making sure that the forms are completed and returned. If all forms are not received, the new accounts processor must notify the account executive that some of the documents are missing. Sometimes a second set must be sent to the client. Good relations between the sales assistant and the customer can often prevent these problems. Good relations between the sales assistant and the new accounts processor insure a smooth operation.

At the end of each day, the new accounts processor prepares a list of new accounts and name and/or address changes and gives it to the CRT operator for transmission to the new accounts department in the home office. This process, often known as NOW (Name and Address Over the Wire), insures that all confirmations of each day's trades will be mailed to the correct name and address.

Switchboard Operator/Receptionist

Most branch offices employ a switchboard operator/receptionist. The receptionist makes the initial contact with any client who calls or visits the firm and makes an important first impression. The receptionist should know which employees are in or out of the office at all times. A caller who was put on hold only to be told that Mr. Smith was out for the day would be annoyed, and rightly so.

If the switchboard operator/receptionist knows who is available, phone calls and other business may be handled more smoothly. An incoming phone call for a vacationing account executive can be answered, "Ms. Jones is on vacation. I will put you through to Mr. Martin, who is covering for her."

You Are Important

Sales assistants and all other branch personnel have one imperative goal: to assist in the generation of revenue for the firm. Your position in the branch either directly or indirectly involves you in activities which are crucial to the generation of revenue needed for branch survival: the opening of new accounts and the servicing of existing accounts. In basic terms, your position in the structure of your office can greatly affect the profits that it generates. The more effectively you handle your responsibilities in concert with your branch colleagues, the more success the firm and *you* will enjoy.

QUIZ 1:1
━━━━━━━━━━━━━━━━━━━━━
Your Position as Sales Assistant

For each question circle the letter next to the best response.

1. The responsibility for serving client accounts resides with the:
   a. Branch manager
   b. Sales assistant
   c. Account executive
   d. Branch cashier
   e. All of the above

2. Assisting the account executive in such activities as posting the book, giving quotes to clients, and verifying transactions is the:
   a. CRT operator
   b. Cashier
   c. Sales assistant
   d. New account processor
   e. Margin clerk

3. The individual at the branch office responsible for the transmission of orders and messages as well as other communications between the branch and the home office is the:
   a. CRT operator
   b. Receptionist
   c. Margin clerk
   d. Cashier
   e. Sales assistant

4. Securities and funds received at the branch office are booked for processing by the:
   a. CRT operator
   b. Cashier
   c. Margin clerk
   d. New account processor
   e. Sales assistant

5. The individual at the branch office responsible for insuring that clients have satisfied all obligations resulting from trading activity is the:
   a. Sales assistant
   b. Branch manager
   c. Margin clerk
   d. Cashier
   e. CRT operator

6. Responsibility for insuring that new accounts are opened in accordance with regulatory and firm requirements rests with the:
   a. New accounts processor
   b. Margin clerk
   c. Cashier
   d. Sales assistant
   e. All of the above

QUIZ ANSWERS 1:1

Your Position as Sales Assistant

1. e. Although primary responsibility lies with the account executive, each of the branch personnel is responsible for insuring that clients receive the best possible service.

2. c. After the account executive, the sales assistant is most familiar with the client and the client's account and service needs.

3. a. The CRT operator is responsible for transmitting and receiving the branch's telecommunicated messages.

4. b. The cashier is responsible for the "booking" (recording) of all securities and funds received at the branch.

5. c. The margin person in the branch has this responsibility. Deficiencies are noted on the "items due list" which is distributed to the account executives each morning.

6. a. The responsibility for making sure that each new account is opened properly, that is to say, that *all* of the required forms have been completed and are in the receipt of the firm, lies with the new accounts processor.

EXERCISE 1:1
The Organizational Structure of Your Branch

Ask your Branch (office/operations) Manager for a copy of your branch's organizational chart. If he or she cannot provide one, ask for his or her assistance in preparing one in the space below. For each position on the organizational chart, be sure to write in the name(s) of the individual(s) holding the position.

Because your branch's organization may well differ from those shown in this lesson's Figures 1-1, 1-2, and 1-3; you should review *your* branch's organizational chart with your account executive. Be sure to discuss the major responsibilities of each position, including how each one interrelates with your function as sales assistant.

BRANCH ORGANIZATIONAL CHART

EXERCISE 1:2 ▬▬▬▬▬▬▬▬▬▬▬▬▬▬▬▬
Your Specific Responsibilities and Duties

The work of the sales assistant varies from branch to branch and sometimes even within the same branch. To help ensure that you and your account executive are in complete agreement on your particular responsibilities and duties, please fill out the following checklist by:

1. Entering a check mark in the appropriate column for each item listed.

2. Adding, in the spaces provided, any additional responsibilities and duties pertinent to your position.

Afterwards, you and your account executive should go through the list, item by item, to ensure that there are no misunderstandings relative to your job responsibilities and duties.

Responsibilities and Duties	Yes	No	Not Sure
1. Accept incoming calls from clients.	____	____	____
2. Respond to client questions about their accounts	____	____	____
3. Verify the accuracy of trades.	____	____	____
4. Insure that new accounts or account changes are processed promptly.	____	____	____
5. Assist the new accounts processor when new accounts are first opened as well as when they must be updated.	____	____	____
6. Work with the margin function to expedite minor customer violations.	____	____	____
7. Work with the new accounts function to give or mail new account forms to the client and follow up to ensure correct completion of all forms.	____	____	____
8. Perform secretarial duties: type memos and correspondence, make photocopies, maintain account executive files, etc.	____	____	____

(List any others.)   Yes   No   Not Sure

9. _____. _____ _____ _____

10. _____. _____ _____ _____

11. _____. _____ _____ _____

12. _____. _____ _____ _____

13. _____. _____ _____ _____

14. _____. _____ _____ _____

15. _____. _____ _____ _____

16. _____. _____ _____ _____

17. _____. _____ _____ _____

18. _____. _____ _____ _____

19. _____. _____ _____ _____

20. _____. _____ _____ _____

21. _____. _____ _____ _____

22. _____. _____ _____ _____

23. _____. _____ _____ _____

24. _____. _____ _____ _____

25. _____. _____ _____ _____

Communication:
The Secret to Effective Telephone Use

To a large extent, your firm's profitability and success depend on you and your ability to professionally and accurately communicate to clients. Few of your firm's clients will actually come into your branch office, but most will use the telephone to effect transactions that can generate substantial revenues for your branch. Consequently, your ability to properly use the telephone is of utmost importance. After all, to the caller your voice and telephone manner constitute the image or impression he or she is getting of your firm. Is it businesslike and professional? Does it inspire confidence and trust?

Naturally, the telephone will not be your only means of communicating with clients. Written correspondence is also important and requires the same high level of professionalism and accuracy. Once again, the image of the firm is at stake. To the prospect or client receiving correspondence from you, each letter is a direct reflection of your firm. In essence, *it is imperative that all of your communication properly reflect your firm's dedication to servicing its clientele in a courteous and professional manner.*

We'll examine the basic principles of communicating by telephone in this lesson and written correspondence in the next.

Using the Telephone

Basic Principles of Telephone Usage

1. Answer the phone immediately. Otherwise an important caller may get discouraged and hang up. Assume *all* calls are important to your branch's profitability.

2. Use a tone of voice that conveys "We're happy to hear from you." Your telephone "attitude" should be one of helpfulness. To the caller *you are the firm*.

3. Pronounce each syllable clearly and pay particular attention to word endings.

4. Strike a happy medium; don't speak too quickly or too slowly, too loudly or too softly. But avoid a monotone delivery. No one wants to talk to a "computer voice."

5. When taking a call at the switchboard or your desk, answer, "This is (name of your firm) good (morning or afternoon)." Similarly, when placing a call identify yourself and your company or department.

6. Always ask for the name of the calling party.

7. If you are at someone else's desk answer:

"Mr. Jones' office, Ms. Gray speaking."

or

"I'm sorry, Mr. Jones has stepped away from his desk, may I have him return the call or perhaps I could help you?"

or

"He's on another line at the moment. He should be busy for about (indicate how long). Would you care to hold?"

or

"He has someone in his office. May I help you?"

or

"I expect him back in about (indicate how long), may I take a message?"

or

"He'll be in a meeting until (indicate time). I'll ask him to call you if you like."

8. Frequently check back with callers when they are on hold. *Never leave anyone on hold for more than 30 seconds without checking back.* To do otherwise may convey to the caller that you (and your firm) do not care about his or her business. If you must leave your desk to gather information, tell your caller how long you'll be gone and offer to call back. If he or she decides to wait, return as quickly as possible and immediately resume the conversation. *The need for courtesy and professionalism cannot be overstated*.

9. Listen intently to the caller. Avoid distractions and focus entirely on what he or she is saying. This will limit the possibility of annoying the caller by asking him or her to repeat something you should have heard.

10. When transferring a call, give the caller the name of the person to whom he or she is being connected. If the call is disconnected, the caller will know whom to call back.

11. Always be polite yet firm when screening calls. Find out the caller's identity and purpose.

12. If both you and your account executive will be out of the office at the same time and the calls would ordinarily come to you, tell your switchboard operator:

● Where you can be reached;
● How long you will be out of the office;
● When you expect to return.

13. Use names and titles frequently: "Mr. and Mrs.," "Dr.," "Judge," and so on. Callers want to be treated with respect, and most find it pleasing to hear their name spoken by someone else.

14. Be careful how you explain a person's absence. Be discreet. You might say, "Mrs. Edwards is out on an appointment, may I have her call you when she returns?"

15. Take concise, complete and accurate messages and pass them along as quickly as possible. Your messages should always include:

● First and last name (check the spelling);
● Telephone number;
● Time of call;
● Message;
● Your signature (in case there is a question).

16. Return all calls promptly.

17. On long distance calls, specify that you are calling long distance since this will increase your chances of a prompt response from the appropriate party. The person-to-person call may be the best bet for the particularly elusive person.

18. Conclude all incoming calls in a cordial manner. Some examples:

To an inquiry:
"Thank you for calling (your company)."

To a repeat caller:
"It's been a pleasure speaking with you again."

To close a service call:
"Thank you for bringing this to our attention. I hope that I've been of service to you."

or

"If there is anything else I could do for you, please let me know."

19. Whenever you want your outgoing calls returned, leave your name and *phone number*. The few seconds it takes to leave your number saves the person you called the inconvenience of having to look it up.

20. Keep an alphabetized list of frequently called numbers.

QUIZ 2:1
Basic Principles of Telephone Usage

For each item write the appropriate response in the space provided.

1. If the phone is not answered immediately, the caller may _____ and the firm may well lose _____.

2. Your telephone "attitude" should convey _____.

3. Never leave a caller on hold for more than _____ seconds without checking back.

4. Your frequent use of a caller's name and/or title will make him or her feel _____.

5. When you take a phone message be sure to get:

    a. _____

    b. _____

    c. _____

    d. _____

6. You need to sign your messages because the people getting them may have _____ about them.

7. After taking a message you should repeat the message to the caller to make sure that it's _____.

8. You should return calls _____.

9. The person-to-person call may be the best way to get through to a particularly _____ person.

10. Incoming calls should be concluded in a _____ manner.

11. When you want your phone call returned, you should leave your name and _____.

QUIZ ANSWERS 2:1

Basic Principles of Telephone Usage

1. If the phone is not answered immediately, the caller may <u>hang up</u> and the firm may well lose <u>revenue</u>, profit, money, etc.

2. Your telephone "attitude" should convey <u>helpfulness</u>.

3. Never leave a caller on hold for more than <u>30</u> seconds without checking back.

4. Your frequent use of a caller's name and/or title will make him or her feel <u>respected</u>, appreciated, warm, good, etc.

5. When you take a phone message be sure to get:
   a. <u>name</u>
   b. <u>phone number</u>
   c. <u>time of call</u>
   d. <u>message</u>

6. You need to sign your messages because the people getting them may have <u>questions</u> about them.

7. After taking a message you should repeat the message to the caller to make sure that it's <u>accurate</u>, correct, etc.

8. You should return calls <u>promptly</u>, immediately, etc.

9. The person-to-person call may be the best way to get through to a particularly <u>elusive</u>, hard-to-get, etc.

10. Incoming calls should be concluded in a <u>cordial</u>, friendly, etc. manner.

11. When you want your phone call returned, you should leave your name and <u>number</u>.

EXERCISE 2:1
━━━━━━━━━━━━━━━━━━━━━━━━━━
Telephone Procedures Unique to Your Branch

See your account executive for answers to the following telephone procedure questions. Enter the appropriate information in the space provided:

1. What should I say when I answer the phone?

_____

2. When you are unavailable, what should I tell the caller?

_____

3. Where do you want me to put your phone messages?

_____

4. What is the procedure for making long distance calls?

_____

5. What is the branch policy regarding making and receiving personal calls?

_____

6. Can you provide me with an index or list of names and numbers that I will call frequently? (Put these names and numbers on a Roll-O-Dex or a similar index which will enable you to retrieve numbers instantly.)

Writing Letters and Memoranda

In order to maintain the public trust and build confidence in firms that act as financial advisors, the New York Stock Exchange provides specific regulations for correspondence to clients. The most important criteria are truthfulness and good taste. Both of these qualities are enhanced by clear and concise writing.

There are exact procedures in each branch office to ensure that these objectives are achieved. The manager must read, initial, and approve each letter that goes out. It is the responsibility of each sales assistant to make sure the branch manager has time to review the outgoing mail. With last minute letters, it is advisable to bring them directly to the branch manager.

Copies of all correspondence must be kept in a file for the periodic review of the compliance auditors. And a separate file must be kept for each account executive by the branch manager's secretary.

Enclosures are also important. Each must be noted in the body or at the bottom of the letter. Many enclosures, for example, a copy of the current prospectus if mutual funds are the subject of the letter, are required by law. These enclosures are provided by the firm. With those that are developed by the account executive, a copy must be filed with the letter after it is approved by the manager. Noting the fact that there is an enclosure and its nature can be quite important if there is a law suit against your firm.

All other contact with clients or the public such as: mailings, reprints of articles, financial reports, advertising, seminars and outside lectures by account executives must be approved by the branch manager.

Guidelines for Effective Communication

There are two aspects to all interoffice and outgoing correspondence. The first has to do with content. What an account executive presents in order to create a favorable impression with clients is of crucial importance. The form in which this message is presented can diminish or enhance its effectiveness. Second, a professional appearance of the communication sends a message of its own. The following are some of the accepted procedures for business correspondence.

Typing

Poorly handled corrections can make any letter look bad. If there is a noticeable correction on a letter, type it over. And make sure the type looks clean and crisp.

Margins

Standard Length Letters. Letters look best when there is a 1¼-inch left-hand margin and a 1-inch right-hand margin. Try to keep the right-hand margin even. However, do not end more than two successive lines with hyphens.

Short Letters. These letters look better when the text is centered on the sheet. This means wider margins on both sides.

Clarity

Correct punctuation, spelling and paragraphing can definitely aid the clarity of the message. Don't hesitate to use available business style reference books and a good dictionary.

The following formatting suggestions will also help. Begin each additional page with a new paragraph. If this is not possible, try to arrange a logical breaking point. However, never carry over the last line of a paragraph to a new page or put the last word of a paragraph on a separate line.

Figure 3-1 shows a sample of a well-written business memorandum.

Figure 3-1. Example of Memo.

MEMORANDUM

Date   April 6, 1986

From   Jim Carlson

To   Louis Chandler

Subject   EXAMPLE of an INTEROFFICE MEMO

Start the first paragraph a triple space from the heading. Do not indent paragraphs.

The title of the sender need not be shown in interoffice memos. Since the sender's name is in the heading, it is not necessary to sign the memo.

Double space if there are fewer than five lines in the memo.

It there is a second page, it should be on similar paper without a heading.

The typist's initials should be flush left and five spaces below the body of the memo.

Enclosures are to be listed two spaces below the initials.

The person(s) to whom copies are to be sent appear two spaces below.

js

Enclosures: Sales Assistant Workbook

cc: Jim White

Guidelines for Business Letters

Date
The date should be placed a double space from the bottom of heading of company logo. The month should be spelled out completely. Use a comma between the day and the year. For example: October 24, 1987.

Inside Address
The inside address should be placed five to nine spaces below the date. Use *Mr., Mrs., Miss* or *Ms.* (when marital status is unknown), even if the business title is used.

The exception is when an academic or professional degree follows the name; for example, John M. Jones, M.D., not Doctor Jones, M.D. Address the letter directly to the person who should read it. The place for the business title is the line following the name; however, if the title is short, separate it from the name with a comma, for example, John M. Jones, Vice-President.

Letter to a Firm
There are letters that are addressed to a firm and marked to the attention of an individual. This is done when the individual will not be opening the letter. The attention line can be placed on the line after the firm's name or a double space below the inside address.

Letter to a Department
The department name goes on the line following the firm's name.

Abbreviations
Don't abbreviate the name of the city. Do use the standard state abbreviation.

Salutation
Depending on the relationship, use *Dear Mr. Thomas* or *Dear Jim*. A non-specific salutation would be *Gentlemen:* or *Mesdames:*.

Subject Line
The subject line highlights the letter topic and must agree in format with the attention line.

Body of the Letter

For short letters of under 75 words, use double spacing. Longer letters should use the previously explained paragraphing rules. The second page must have a minimum of three lines from the last paragraph and the complimentary close. The firm's identification should be used as part of the signature block on the second page: for example, Mr. John M. Jones,

Vice-President,

Williams and Company.

It is optional on a one-page letter.

Complimentary Close

The spacing should be set a double space below the body of the letter. *Sincerely Yours,* or *Sincerely,* is popular today. Two spaces below can be the firm's identification line.

Signature Block

The signature block should be placed at least four spaces below the complimentary close or the firm's identification line. First, put the name of the individual who is signing the letter. The signer's title can follow on the same line, separated by a comma, or on the next line.

Identification Line

Place this line a double space below the signature block. If the sender originates the letter use typist's initials. If someone else originates the letter, some follow this format: JRD:MN:tm—*JRD* has signed the letter, *MN* has originated the letter, *tm* has typed the letter.

Enclosure Notation

Place this notation a double space below the identification line. Place the word *Enclosure:* flush left and then list enclosures.

Carbon Copy

Place this notation a double space below the enclosure notation. Place *cc:* flush left and then list people who will receive copies.

Postscript

List this notation a double space below the last notation. At the author's option, the postscript can be handwritten. If it is typed, place the postscript flush left.

Figure 3-2. Example of Business Letter.

September 3, 1986

Mr. Mark Peters, Vice President
Growth Corporation
70 Pine Street
New York, NY 10270

Dear Mr. Peters:

BUSINESS LETTER FORMAT

This is a sample letter that illustrates a popular business letter format. It is clear and effective. It works well with almost any heading. The lack of indentation speeds up the typing process and gives a professional appearance.

It is designed to provide a record of who originated the letter, who authored and signed it, and who typed it. Provision has been made for listing enclosures and the individual(s) to whom copies would be sent.

Sincerely,

Louis Chandler

LC:JKR:mp

Enclosures: Guidelines for Business Letters

cc: Mary Harris

SECTION 4
Opening New Accounts

The Account Executive

The growth of your branch office depends on an expanding service of existing accounts and the opening of new accounts. One of the account executive's major sales activities is directed towards converting prospects into clients. Success in this effort is measured by the number of new accounts.

A very important part of this sales effort is obtaining background information from the client. During the time the account executive is filling out the new account form with the prospective client, he/she is evaluating their investment assets and objectives, and deciding which type of account is proper for them.

When an account executive sets up an account, it must be one best suited for the client's purposes. If there are legal restrictions, the firm and client should become aware of them. Otherwise, a dissatisfied client may take his/her business elsewhere or even file suit against the brokerage firm.

The New York Stock Exchange rules make very clear the responsibilities of the registered representative and the managers of the firm for each new account. The form must be accurate and complete to determine if the firm will do business with this client.

The Sales Assistant

The sales assistant aids the account executive in the efficient opening of new accounts, and the effective processing of the many documents connected with this initial client contact.

This responsibility requires the sales assistant:

- To understand New York Stock Exchange Rule 405;
- To know the New Account Form;
- To be familiar with branch procedures for processing this form, including the necessary documents for the various account categories.

Knowing the Customer

Rule 405 of the New York Stock Exchange (NYSE) provides the guidelines for opening new accounts. This rule designates the responsible parties and their duties.

"Every member organization is required through a general partner, a principal, executive officer or a person or persons designated under provision of Rule 342(b) (1) to:

1. "Use due diligence to learn the essential facts relative to every customer, every order, every cash or margin account holding power of attorney over any account accepted or carried by such organizations."

2. "Supervise diligently all accounts handled by registered representatives of the organization."

3. "Specifically approve the opening of an account prior to or promptly after the completion of any transaction for the account of or with a customer, provided, however, that in the case of branch offices, the opening of such an account for a customer may be approved by the manager of such branch office, but the action of such branch office manager shall, within a reasonable time, be approved by a general partner, a principal executive officer or a person or persons designated under the provision of Rule 342(b) (1). The member, general partner, officer or designated person approving the opening of the account shall, prior to giving his approval, be personally informed as to the essential facts relative to the customer and to the nature of the proposed account, and shall indicate his approval in writing on a document which is part of the permanent records of his office or organization."

Overview

Selecting the most appropriate type of account is a major responsibility for the account executive. Different types of accounts require different forms. The sales assistant must be familiar with the variety of accounts offered by their firm and what documentation must be completed and processed for each of them.

Types of Accounts

Cash Account

The individual cash account is the simplest type of account. With an individual cash account, a client can buy and/or sell securities. Industry rules require that most purchases must be paid for within five business days, but no later than the seventh business day. A client has only to give the information required for a new account form to open this type of account. Thus, it can be opened over the phone.

Margin Account

In order to borrow money from the firm to buy securities, a client must open a margin account. Those clients who want to sell short or enter into certain types of option transactions are required to maintain margin accounts. To establish this type of account, the client must sign a margin account agreement, and, at most firms, a lending agreement. The client must also provide the information for the new account form. Purchases must be paid for by the fifth business day.

Joint Account

There are two types of joint accounts entailing ownership by two or more people. The accounts differ in what happens when one of the owners dies. In the case of joint tenants with rights of survivorship (JTWROS), the account becomes the full property of the survivor(s). A tenants in common account (TCOM or TIC) is such that if one of the parties dies, his/her interest passes to the estate, unless some other arrangement has been made.

Discretionary Account

A discretionary account must be authorized in writing by the client and approved by the firm's management. Such accounts permit the broker to sell securities and to reinvest the proceeds according to the investment objectives of the client. The broker makes the choice of the securities that are to be bought and sold. All orders must be marked *discretionary* and reviewed by the branch manager. The account executive operates the account under the provisions of NYSE Rule 408. It is an industry rule that states that whenever an account is operated by another person, either a full or limited power of attorney is required.

Custodian Accounts

These accounts are opened for a minor. They operate under the Uniform Gift to Minors Act. All funds and securities belong to the minor and not the adult operating it. Securities transferred out of the account, as well as checks drawn on it, must carry the full name of the account. The custodian must be reasonable in the conduct of the account and, in general, make only conservative investments.

Trust Accounts

Trusts may also be established for the benefit of individuals. The trust may take effect after the death of the giver (testamentary trust), or while the donor is still alive (inter vivos trust). When trust accounts are opened, a trust agreement form must be completed and a copy of the trust itself must be supplied to the firm.

Partnership Accounts

In these accounts, two or more individuals enter into an agreement to invest in securities. The partnership may be an ongoing business under law or set up for the purpose of investing. The names of all the partners, the distribution of assets, investment purposes, and the account management must be specified. A copy of the partnership agreement must be filed together with the new account and partnership forms.

Investment Clubs

Investment clubs may be organized by informal agreements among individuals to contribute a fixed sum each month to purchase securities, or they may result from formal agreements, with written rules and officers who manage the account. The club should take care of its own recordkeeping and order placing. The firm should concentrate solely on servicing the account itself. In fact, many firms do not permit their employees to organize investment clubs—only to be their brokers.

Institutional Accounts

These accounts will be explained in greater detail in Lesson Six. Institutional accounts include:

Corporate Accounts. Copies of the corporate charter and/or bylaws, and corporate resolution must be filed with the new account form. The charter will specify the type of business the corporation is permitted to transact and the resolution lists the persons who are empowered to act on the corporation's behalf.

Pension Funds, Bank-Manager Trusts. The legal departments of these professional entities will complete the new account form and provide the required documentation.

Usually institutional type accounts are Delivery Versus Payment (DVP) accounts. The delivery instructions become part of the "standing instructions" and may specify a bank that is being used as an agent by the client. Agent banks using a depository such as Depository Trust Company (DTC) and electronic institutional delivery (ID) service must establish this when opening, or updating, an account by providing its "FINS" number.

Option Accounts

This account will be explained in greater detail in Lesson Seven.

To trade in options, an account must provide special documentation. Options are not suitable for all accounts. A new client must help to complete an option information form and must return a signed option agreement after reviewing a copy of the Option Clearing Corporation risk disclosure document. Option accounts require a special approval of a Registered Options Principal (ROP)—usually the office manager—before any trades are permitted in the account.

Commodity Futures Accounts

Futures are traded in a separate account, for which appropriate documents must be completed. To establish a commodity account the client must complete a commodity suitability form and sign the suitability letter. To permit transfer of funds between a client's security and commodity accounts the client must also complete a transfer of funds form.

Direct Access Account

A new type of account is one that combines the security account with a checking account and a credit card service giving instant access to funds. Such accounts are known by different names.

Other Types of Accounts

Community Property Account. Account of husband and wife in Community Property states.

Sole Proprietorship. Account of an unincorporated business owned by one person (and his/her) spouse.

Unincorporated Association. Account of an association of people formed for non-business purposes.

Accounts for an Educational Institution or Nonprofit/Charitable Organization or Religious Group.

Numbered Account. Account that uses a number for identification instead of owner's name/address.

Mutual Fund Account. Account of an Investment Company that is registered with the SEC.

Hedge Fund. Account of a limited partnership whose purpose is investments and operates under NYSE rules.

Accounts for a Banking Institution, Insurance Company, Listed Company, or Government Agency.

ERISA Account. Corporate employee benefits account.

IRA Account. Individual retirement. Firm as custodian.

Keogh Account. Self-employed person's retirement account. Firm as custodian.

Accounts for a Testamentary Trust (U/W/O; that is, under the will of . . .), Estate Account (Testate), Estate Account (Intestate), or Life Tenant (U/W/O).

Accounts for a Court Appointed Guardianship, Conservatorship, or Committee.

Summary

Each sales assistant who is involved with the processing of new accounts should become familiar with all of the forms required by the firm, the accounts to which they apply, and what documents are needed if changes are made. This will increase the efficiency of the operation and the satisfaction of the client.

In Figure 4-1, we have given a sample of a new account form from one member firm. Other firms have similar forms and there is no standard form. The best exercise for a new sales assistant is to obtain such a form from his/her firm and to complete it.

Figure 4-1. A Typical New Account Form.

*ALES Assistant— GET A NEW ACCOUNT FORM FROM THE BACK OFFICE,
FOLLOW THE INSTRUCTIONS ON YOUR COMPANY'S FORM.*

NEW ACCOUNT APPLICATION AND OPTION SUITABILITY

1. Branch no.	Client no.	T	C	AE no.

2. Types of account CASH MARGIN COMMOD COM OPT	3. Social security no. Fed. tax ID no.

| 4. Cash   MAIL   HOLD
distributions _____	5. TEFRA—Check box if exempt.

6. Locator code	7. Zip	8. IRA/SEP/Keogh—Check if retirement account.

9. Employee-code	10. Statements—Check if monthly.

11. Legal name and mailing address Home	Business

| 12. Primary account activity name
   MR. _____ MRS. _____ MS. _____ OTHER_____ | 13. Check if employee or
   relation of employee | 14. Date |
|---|---|---|

15. Home telephone number	16. Business telephone number

| 17. Name of employer _____
Address _____	18. Nature of business
	19. Est d annual income	20. Yrs of employment
	21. Occupation

| 22. Spouse's name _____
Occupation	24. Bank reference/name and address _____
23. Spouse's employer _____
Address _____	List checking and savings account numbers _____
VERIFIED? YES _____ NO _____

25. Other brokerage firm accounts? YES _____ NO _____ List firm(s)_____

26. US Citizen YES NO	27. Marital status MARRIED SINGLE DIVORCED WIDOWED	28. Date of birth

29. Number of dependents	30. Home OWN RENT

31. Does client or other member of household have other accounts with us?
ACCOUNT NUMBERS

| 32. Investment objectives

INCOME WITH SAFETY _____ INCOME WITH RISK _____
APPRECIATION WITH SAFETY _____ TAX REDUCTION _____
APPRECIATION WITH RISK _____
SPECULATIVE | 33. Net worth information

ESTIMATED TAXES _____
ESTIMATED LIQUID WORTH _____
ESTIMATE TOTAL NET WORTH |
|---|---|

34. Initial transaction PURCHASE SALE OTHER	35. Initial deposit

(cont.)

Figure 4-1. (cont.)

36. Asset review (indicate client's present holdings and amount of each)

CDs _____	PREFERRED STOCKS _____
STOCKS _____	MUNICIPAL BONDS _____
RULE 144/145 Secs._____	UNIT TRUSTS _____
OPTIONS _____	MONEY FUNDS _____
COMMODITIES/FUTURES _____	ANNUITIES _____
PRECIOUS METALS/COINS _____	TAX SHELTERS _____
NONHOME REAL ESTATE _____	REAL ESTATE PARTNERSHIP _____
GOVERNMENT BONDS_____	WHOLE LIFE _____ TERM _____
GNMAs _____	HEALTH _____ DISABILITY _____
CORPORATE BONDS _____	TREASURES _____ OTHER _____

37. Client's corporate position—*Is the client now or has he/she ever been a corporate officer or own 10 percent of corporation stock?*   YES _____ NO _____

38. Same state registration—*Is AE registered in the same state as client's residence?*   YES _____ NO _____

39. Discretionary authorization   YES _____ NO _____
If discretion is granted, specify agent's name/address.

40. AE's signature (no initials)   Date _____

41. Has client been provided a risk disclosure statement?

       YES _____ NO _____

Has client previously traded equity options?   YES_____ NO _____ If yes, how long? _____
Buyer: _____ Seller: _____
Are equity options suitable for investment objectives?   YES _____ NO _____
Is client aware of financial risks of equity options?   YES _____ NO _____
Equity option activity anticipated: _____
Has client previously traded debt options?   YES _____ NO _____ If yes, how long? _____
Buyer: _____ Seller: _____
Are debt options suitable for investment objectives?   YES_____ NO _____
Is client aware of financial risk of debt options?   YES _____ NO _____
Debt option activity anticipated: _____
_____

42. ROP's signature (option approval)   Date

43. Branch manager's approval   Date

New Account Application Form

Retail Customers Only

1. Account Number

Branch No.	Client No.	T	C	AE No.
. .	. . .			. .

Generally, the new accounts processor in the home office provides an account number after the new account application form is completed by the account executive and approved by the branch manager.

2. Types of Accounts

[ ] Cash [ ] Margin [ ] Commodity [ ] Option
[ ] Commodity Option

The account executive checks off at least one of these types after finding out the type of business the client intends to transact.

3. Social Security or Federal Taxpayer Identification Number

[ ] Social Security No. [ ] Fed. Tax ID Number	Social Security or Fed. Tax ID No. . . . .

U.S. Treasury Department regulation 103.35 requires one of these identification numbers to be entered on the right.
There is a foreign client exception for non-U.S. citizens who derive no income in the United States.

4. Dividends/Interest

[ ] Mail Cash distribution [ ] Hold Cash distribution

The client decides if they want a check for their dividends mailed to them immediately, or once a month, or to have the dividends held in their account.

5. Tax Equity and Fiscal Responsibility Act (TEFRA).

[ ] Check box if exempt from TEFRA

Exempt accounts must confirm their taxpayer's number by signing the W-9 TEFRA form.
These are the exemptions:

- A simple trust. All beneficiaries must be exempt individuals, organizations, or retirement plans.
- A common trust fund, or a tax-exempt trust, or a real estate investment trust.

- A corporation.
- A financial institution.
- A tax-exempt organization.
- An individual retirement plan.
- A securities or commodities dealer.
- An entity registered under the Investment Company Act of 1940.
- A middleman between the payer and payee. This will include a nominee or custodian.
- Government entities including: The U.S. Government, a U.S. agency, a State, the District of Columbia, a U.S. possession, or the political subdivisions of these entities.
- A foreign government and its political subdivisions, wholly-owned agencies, or instrumentalities.
- An international organization or its wholly-owned agencies and instrumentalities.
- A foreign central bank.

6. *Geographical Code.* Geographical Code for non-U.S. residents ensures the correct dividend withholding tax for nonresidents.

7. *Postal Zip Code.* Essential to transmission over the wire and the efficient handling of correspondence.

8. *IRA/SEP/Keogh.* Check box if this is a retirement account.

9. *Employee Code.* Check box if client is an employee of the firm.

10. *Statements.* Check box if client wants statements sent monthly. Otherwise they will be sent quarterly or if there is activity during the month.

11. *Legal Name and Mailing Address.* Must be the correct names of the account. The mailing address should be a permanent residence. A post office box and/or a temporary address is generally unacceptable.

12. *Primary Account Activity Name.* Check correct box.

[ ] Mr.   [ ] Mrs.   [ ] Ms.   [ ] Specify other title.

Other titles might be Doctor, Captain, Reverend, etc.

13. *Employee or Employee Related.* Check box if this applies.

14. *Date.* Enter the opening date of the account.

15. Home Telephone Number. This must be provided even if unlisted. Include area code.

16. Business Telephone Number. The purpose is to maintain client contact. Initially, it can be used to verify employment.

17. Employer's Name and Address. Must be complete and accurate.

18. Nature of Business. Note carefully if the client is an employee of a bank, insurance company or brokerage firm. Their employer must give your firm its written permission before they can open a MARGIN account. Those clients who work for brokerage firms must provide written permission to open ANY account.

19. Estimated Annual Income. Necessary to decide on which types of investments are most suitable for the client.

20. Years Employed. Limit this information to present employer.

21. Occupation. Find out what the client's position/title is, or was before retirement. It is important to know if the client is, or was, an officer, director or controlling stockholder of a public corporation.

22. Spouse's Name, Occupation, Annual Income. To know your customer and, if necessary, to do a credit check, it's important to have this information about a married client.

23. Spouse's Employer and Address. This information is necessary whether the account is single or joint. Prior written permission must be obtained if the spouse is employed by a bank, insurance company or brokerage firm and the couple went to open a joint margin account.

24. Bank Reference. The name and complete mailing address of the client's bank must be entered on the form. Also enter the type of bank account. Indicate if the information has been verified. All of this is important if a credit check is necessary.

25. Other Brokerage Accounts. If there is another account, enter the firm's name, or check the *No* box. Employees of other brokerage firms MUST furnish this information.

26. Citizenship. Indicate if the client is a U.S. citizen. If not, enter country of citizenship. This is required by law due to restrictions on foreign ownership of certain securities and rules about dividend withholding tax. If the client is not a U.S. citizen but is a resident alien, the client will have a green card permitting his/her permanent residency. Do not hesitate to ask to see this card. The greed card signifies, among other things, that the applicant is governed by the tax laws of the United States.

27. Marital Status. Married? Single? Divorced? Widowed? One item must be checked.

28. Date of Birth. Clients must be of legal age. Suitability for certain types of business is also a consideration. The exact date is the only acceptable entry.

29. Number of Dependents. Enter the number.

30. Home.

[ ] Own [ ] Rent

Check one box. This is also one insight into the client's net worth.

31. Other Accounts. Does the client or some other member of the household have an account(s) with your firm? Enter the account number. Could be a joint, trust or retirement account.

32. Investment Objectives. Check one or more.

[ ] Income with safety   [ ] Appreciation with safety
[ ] Income with risk   [ ] Appreciation with risk
[ ] Tax reduction   [ ] Speculation

The box checked should be the best indication of proper investments for the client. As a general rule, the three boxes to the right are for investments in stocks; the three boxes to the left for bonds.

33. Net Worth Information

Estimated Annual Household Income—A strong indication of client's suitability for certain investments.

Estimated Annual Taxes—Important in deciding on current investment strategy.

Estimated Liquid Net Worth—This is easily accessible money such as cash, money in certain bank accounts etc.

Estimated Total Net Worth—All of a client's assets minus debts equals total net worth.

34. Initial Transaction. Purchase, sale or other. If "other," specify type of business.

35. Initial Deposit. If the first transaction is a purchase, indicate the amount of money that was deposited. In the case of a sale indicate the number of shares and security name.

36. Assets Review. Enter dollar amounts of each asset. This information is essential in analyzing the client's financial position. Include all financial assets: CDs, stocks, bonds, real estate investments, commodities/futures, precious metals/coins, and so on.

37. Client's Corporate Position. Should the client be a corporate officer, now or in the past, or own 10 percent of a corporation stock, check the YES box and specify the corporation. Otherwise check the NO box.

38. Same State Registration. The account executive must be registered in the same state as the client's residence. Check the "Yes" box to indicate that this is the case. The new accounts processor will verify this fact. Not all firms have such an entry. Instead they require the registered representative to make sure this registration is valid.

39. Discretionary Authorization. If someone other than the client; for example, an agent, is authorized to transact business for the client, check the YES box and enter the full name and address of this individual. If this is not the case, check the NO box.

40. Account Executive's Signature. After the application has been checked, the account executive signs his/her complete name. Initials are not acceptable.

41. Option Section. This section is to determine a client's option suitability. If the client intends to trade options, each question must be answered and the client must be provided with a *Risk Disclosure Statement.* This is also true of a client with an existing account if he/she decides to trade options.

- *Risk Disclosure Statement*—The firm has the responsibility to provide the client with the risk disclosure statement prior to, or not later than, the date of the first option trade. The date the client receives this document must be entered on the application.

- *Equity Options and Anticipated Activity, and Debt Options and Anticipated Activity*—Questions about previous experience, awareness of risk, suitability for investment objectives and types of anticipated activity must all be answered in this option section.

42. Registered Option Principal (ROP) Signature. If the client intends to trade options, the application must be approved by a ROP. The branch manager is usually a ROP. If this is not the case, New York Option Compliance can give approval after reviewing the application. The signature must be a full name. No nicknames, please.

43. Branch Manager Signature. After reviewing the application, the branch manager indicates approval by signing his/her full name.

Figure 4-2. New Account Form Filled Out.

NEW ACCOUNT APPLICATION AND OPTION SUITABILITY

1. Branch no. *200*	Client no. *1246*	T *1*	C *6*	AE no. *034*

2. Types of account CASH ✓ MARGIN COMMOD COM OPT	3. Social security no. Fed. tax ID no. *247372641*

4 Cash distributions MAIL HOLD	5. TEFRA—Check box if exempt.

6. Locator code	7. Zip *06850*	8. IRA/SEP/Keogh—Check if retirement account.

9. Employee-code	10. Statements—Check if monthly.

11. Legal name and mailing address *MR. PHILLIP THOMAS* Home *29 VAN BUREN AVE, NORWALK, CT.*	Business

12. Primary account activity name MR. ✓ MRS. ____ MS. ____ OTHER ____	13. Check if employee or relation of employee	14. Date *9-3-8X*

15. Home telephone number *(203) 836-4687*	16. Business telephone number *(203) 742-5372*

17. Name of employer *DATA SKILLS, INC,* Address *32 DARBY DRIVE COS COB, CT.*	18. Nature of business *COMPUTER*
	19. Est'd annual income *86 M* 20. Yrs of employment *4*
	21. Occupation *MARKETING*

22. Spouse's name *PHYLLIS* Occupation *HOMEMAKER* 23. Spouse's employer Address	24. Bank reference/name and address *CONNECTICUT BANK & TRUST Co. 200 MAIN ST., NORWALK, CT.* List checking and savings account numbers VERIFIED? YES ✓ NO ____

25. Other brokerage firm accounts? YES ✓ NO ____ List firm(s) *E F HUTTON*

26. US Citizen YES ✓ NO	27. Marital status MARRIED ✓ SINGLE DIVORCED WIDOWED	28. Date of birth *4/20/40*

29. Number of dependents *3*	30. Home OWN ✓ RENT

31. Does client or other member of household have other accounts with us? ACCOUNT NUMBERS

32. Investment objectives INCOME WITH SAFETY ✓ INCOME WITH RISK ____ APPRECIATION WITH SAFETY ____ TAX REDUCTION ____ APPRECIATION WITH RISK ____ SPECULATIVE	33. Net worth information *ESTIMATED ANN'L INC. 90M* ESTIMATED TAXES *25M* ESTIMATED LIQUID WORTH *40M* ESTIMATE TOTAL NET WORTH *400M*

34. Initial transaction PURCHASE ✓ SALE OTHER	35. Initial deposit

(cont.)

45

Figure 4-2. (cont.)

36. Asset review (indicate client's present holdings and amount of each)

CDs _____ 40M _____	PREFERRED STOCKS _____
STOCKS _____	MUNICIPAL BONDS _____
RULE 144/145 Secs. _____	UNIT TRUSTS _____
OPTIONS _____	MONEY FUNDS _____ 60M _____
COMMODITIES/FUTURES _____	ANNUITIES _____
PRECIOUS METALS/COINS _____	TAX SHELTERS _____
NONHOME REAL ESTATE _____	REAL ESTATE PARTNERSHIP _____
GOVERNMENT BONDS _____	WHOLE LIFE _____ TERM _____
GNMAs _____	HEALTH _____ DISABILITY _____
CORPORATE BONDS _____	TREASURES _____ OTHER _____

37. Client's corporate position—*Is the client now or has he/she ever been a corporate officer or own 10 percent of corporation stock?*
    YES _____ NO ✔

38. Same state registration—*Is AE registered in the same state as client's residence?*
    YES ✔ NO _____

39. Discretionary authorization   YES _____ NO ✔
    If discretion is granted, specify agent's name/address.

40. AE's signature (no initials)   Date _9/3/8X_
    Robert Holmes

41. Has client been provided a risk disclosure statement?
    YES _____ NO _____

Has client previously traded equity options?   YES _____ NO _____ If yes, how long? _____
Buyer: _____ Seller: _____
Are equity options suitable for investment objectives?   YES _____ NO _____
Is client aware of financial risks of equity options?   YES _____ NO _____
Equity option activity anticipated: _____
Has client previously traded debt options?   YES _____ NO _____ If yes, how long? _____
Buyer: _____ Seller: _____
Are debt options suitable for investment objectives?   YES _____ NO _____
Is client aware of financial risk of debt options?   YES _____ NO _____
Debt option activity anticipated: _____

42. ROP's signature (option approval)   Date

43. Branch manager's approval   Date _9/3/8X_
    Samuel Brown

EXERCISE: 4:1
New Account Application

Fill out the new account application form for the client information listed below.

List the documents that are required if this client wants to open:

1. A joint account:

_____

_____

_____

2. A trust account:

_____

_____

_____

If the client works for a bank, what document is required?

_____

Put an information not available (N/A is a commonly accepted abbreviation) in any answer area where you do not have the facts.

Client Profile

Harry Richards, SS# 156-62-8954, aged 40, DOB: June 7, 1946*
Client wants to open a cash account with a monthly statement.
Engineer, EXP Corporation, 400 South Street, Morristown, NJ, 07960
Income $50,000

Client has never been a corporate officer or owned 10 percent of any corporate stock.

Married. Wife: Helen, Age 34, DOB: July 16, 1952, Loan Officer, City Bank, 126 Main Street, Morristown, NJ, 07960, Income $32,000
Two children—Jill and Jason, ages 9 and 7.

They are willing to take some risk in their investments. They are not interested in options. For now, they don't want a joint account; so Harry will be the owner.

Bank—Morristown National Bank, checking and saving—$46,000
Has income producing real estate partnership (estimated value $10,000)
Net worth, liquid, $65,000. Total worth—$200,000.

Rent Apartment. Address—780 High Street, Morristown, NJ, 07960.
Home (201) 536-9742, Office (201) 624-6376

Want to buy 300 shares of GM Hold dividends in the account.

*In some firms, the client is asked only if he/she is of age.

Figure 4-3. New Account Form.

NEW ACCOUNT APPLICATION AND OPTION SUITABILITY

1. Branch no.	Client no.	T	C	AE no.

2. Types of account CASH MARGIN COMMOD COM OPT	3. Social security no. Fed. tax ID no.

4. Cash Distributions MAIL HOLD	5. TEFRA—Check box if exempt.

6. Locator code	7. Zip	8. IRA/SEP/Keogh—Check if retirement account.

9. Employee code	10. Statements—Check if monthly.

11. Legal name and mailing address Home	Business

| 12. Primary account activity name
MR. _____ MRS. _____ MS. _____ OTHER_____	13. Check if employee or relation of employee	14. Date

15. Home telephone number	16. Business telephone number

| 17. Name of employer _____
Address _____	18. Nature of business
	19. Est d annual income	20. Yrs of employment
	21. Occupation

| 22. Spouse's name _____
Occupation	24. Bank reference/name and address _____
23. Spouse's employer _____
Address _____	List checking and savings account numbers _____
	VERIFIED? YES _____ NO _____

25. Other brokerage firm accounts? YES ____ NO ____ List firm(s)_____

26. US Citizen YES NO	27. Marital status MARRIED SINGLE DIVORCED WIDOWED	28. Date of birth

29. Number of dependents	30. Home OWN RENT

31. Does client or other member of household have other accounts with us?
ACCOUNT NUMBERS

| 32. Investment objectives

INCOME WITH SAFETY _____ INCOME WITH RISK _____
APPRECIATION WITH SAFETY _____ TAX REDUCTION _____
APPRECIATION WITH RISK _____
SPECULATIVE | 33. Net worth information

ESTIMATED TAXES _____
ESTIMATED LIQUID WORTH _____
ESTIMATE TOTAL NET WORTH |
|---|---|
| 34. Initial transaction   PURCHASE   SALE   OTHER | 35. Initial deposit |

(cont.)

Figure 4-3. (cont.)

36. Asset review (indicate client's present holdings and amount of each)

CDs _____	PREFERRED STOCKS _____
STOCKS _____	MUNICIPAL BONDS _____
RULE 144/145 Secs. _____	UNIT TRUSTS _____
OPTIONS _____	MONEY FUNDS _____
COMMODITIES/FUTURES _____	ANNUITIES _____
PRECIOUS METALS/COINS _____	TAX SHELTERS _____
NONHOME REAL·ESTATE _____	REAL ESTATE PARTNERSHIP _____
GOVERNMENT BONDS _____	WHOLE LIFE _____ TERM _____
GNMAs _____	HEALTH _____ DISABILITY _____
CORPORATE BONDS _____	TREASURES _____ OTHER _____

37. Client's corporate position—*Is the client now or has he/she ever been a corporate officer or own 10 percent of corporation stock?*
  YES _____ NO _____

38. Same state registration—*Is AE registered in the same state as client's residence?*
  YES _____ NO _____

39. Discretionary authorization   YES _____ NO _____
  If discretion is granted, specify agent's name/address.

40. AE's signature (no initials)   Date _____

41. Has client been provided a risk disclosure statement?
  YES _____ NO _____

  Has client previously traded equity options?   YES _____ NO _____ If yes, how long? _____
  Buyer: _____ Seller: _____
  Are equity options suitable for investment objectives?   YES _____ NO _____
  Is client aware of financial risks of equity options?   YES _____ NO _____
  Equity option activity anticipated: _____
  Has client previously traded debt options?   YES _____ NO _____ If yes, how long? _____
  Buyer: _____ Seller: _____
  Are debt options suitable for investment objectives?   YES _____ NO _____
  Is client aware of financial risk of debt options?   YES _____ NO _____
  Debt option activity anticipated: _____
  _____

42. ROP's signature (option approval)   Date

43. Branch manager's approval   Date

The Paper Trail for Opening a New Account

First, the account executive completes the form and signs it. The sales assistant aids the account executive in processing the application and in obtaining the documents that are necessary to open the account.

Here are the steps for what happens next when opening a typical new account.

Step One

The account executive must ask about every general item on the form unless it is obvious that the information is not relevant. With the client, the account executive enters all of the required information including the client's investment strategy. (The account executive is especially attentive to applications of clients who want to trade in options or commodities.)

Industry rules do not require extensive questions if the client is about to sell fully-owned securities in a *one-time* sale. For example, a client, with no other security holdings, wants to sell 30 shares of Tenneco with a market value of $1,300. The questioning can be abbreviated provided the client establishes identity, ownership, and has the shares in hand. Such sales should *never* be made over the phone.

Step Two

The account executive or the sales assistant makes sure all of the information is accurate, the bank account is verified and all of the necessary documents for the type of new account the client wants are completed and in the branch. If everything passes inspection, the account executive should sign the application and take it to the branch manager for approval.

Step Three

After reviewing the new account application form, the branch manager must sign it to indicate approval.

Step Four

A new account number is assigned by the new accounts clerk. The new accounts clerk must be informed if a special range of account numbers is required. A typical account number may consist of as many as 13 digits:

Branch Number	Client Number	Type	Check Digit	Account Exec. No.
000	12345	1	2	345

This will vary from firm to firm. The bottom copy of the form is returned to the sales assistant for the account executive's records. As you can see, the client number can tell you a lot about the account.

Step Five

At the end of each day, the new accounts processor prepares a list of new accounts and name and/or address changes and gives it to the CRT operator for transmission to the new accounts department at the home office. This process insures that all confirmations of each day's trades will be mailed to the correct name and address.

Step Six

After the transmission, a copy is provided to the account executive to be verified. Should there be errors, they must be reported promptly to the new accounts clerk for correction right away. If an order had been executed that day, correction must be made at once so that the client confirmation is correct the next day. Special forms must be used for other than same-day corrections.

Step Seven

Later, the account executive must verify the address and spelling. These records are to be maintained in an account number file for easy client access and back-up. (The account number, rather than the name, identifies all communication with the home office.)

Summary

- Step One—Acquire client information
- Step Two—Verify information and documents
- Step Three—Branch manager review and approval
- Step Four—Account number assigned
- Step Five—"Live" transmission to home office
- Step Six—Verify transmission
- Step Seven—Maintain client record file.

THIS PAGE IS FOR COPY OF A
CLIENT'S AGREEMENT.

Obtain a copy of the Client Agreement for your firm and insert
it here. You may throw out this page, once you have the form.

THIS PAGE IS FOR COPY OF A
W-9 TAX FORM AND INSTRUCTIONS.

QUIZ 4:1
New Account Applications

Instructions: Enter your response in the appropriate spaces.

1. To aid the account executive, the sales assistant should be familiar with:

   • Knowing the customer, NYSE Rule _____.

   • Entering information on the _____ form.

   • The requirements to get _____ approval.

   • The necessary _____ for different types of accounts.

2. The _____ must be verified in case a credit check is necessary.

3. There are six *investment objectives* listed on the application. Name three of these investment objectives:

   • _____

   • _____

   • _____

4. Unless instructed otherwise, when there is no activity in an account, statements will be sent _____.

5. Employees of _____, _____ and _____ must have prior written permission before opening a _____account.

6. Name six types of accounts:

   1. _____
   2. _____
   3. _____
   4. _____
   5. _____
   6. _____

7. Put an "X" next to any of the above accounts that are exempt from TEFRA.

8. *Paper trail*—Briefly describe each of the seven steps in opening a typical new account.

   1. _____

      _____

   2. _____

      _____

3. _____

_____

4. _____

_____

5. _____

_____

6. _____

_____

7. _____

_____

9. What document must be sent to a client if he/she wants to open an option account?

_____

10. Jill Jones works for XYZ Brokerage Firm. What *must* she do before opening any account with ABC Brokerage Firm?

_____

11. Jill Jones is a registered account executive in New York. Her friend Mary Smith lives and works in New Jersey. Can Jill open an account for Mary? Yes_____ No_____

12. Define:

TEFRA _____

UGMA _____

DVP _____

NOW _____

13. *Discretionary account*—Whenever an account is operated by another, either a full or a limited _____ is required.

14. *Custodian account*—The custodian must make only _____ investments.

15. *Joint account*—Describe the difference between the two major types of joint accounts: JTWROS and tenants in common.

_____

_____

NOTE

_____
_____
_____
_____
_____
_____
_____
_____
_____
_____
_____
_____
_____
_____
_____
_____
_____
_____
_____
_____
_____
_____
_____
_____
_____
_____
_____

QUIZ ANSWERS 4:1

New Account Applications

1. To aid the account executive, the sales assistant should be familiar with:
   - Knowing the customer, NYSE Rule <u>405</u>.
   - Entering information on the <u>new account application</u> form.
   - The requirements to get <u>branch manager</u> approval.
   - The necessary <u>documents</u> for different types of accounts.
2. The <u>bank reference</u> must be verified in case a credit check is necessary.
3. There are six *investment objectives* listed on the application. Name three of these investment objectives:
   - <u>Appreciation with safety</u>
   - <u>Appreciation with risk</u>
   - <u>Speculation</u>
   - <u>Income with safety</u>
   - <u>Income with risk</u>
   - <u>Tax Reduction</u>
4. Unless instructed otherwise, when there is no activity in an account statements will be sent <u>quarterly</u>.
5. Employees of <u>banks, insurance companies</u>, and <u>brokerage firms</u> (any account with another firm) must have prior written permission before opening a margin account.
6. Name six types of accounts:

<u>Cash</u> and	<u>Partnership</u>	<u>Commodity</u>
<u>Margin</u>	<u>Investment club</u>	<u>Direct access</u>
<u>Joint (WROS, TCOM)</u>	<u>Corporate</u>	<u>Numbered</u>
<u>Discretionary</u>	<u>Pension fund</u>	<u>Hedge</u>
<u>Custodian</u>	<u>Bank-managed trust</u>	<u>IRA</u>
<u>Trust</u>	<u>Option</u>	<u>Keogh</u>

7. Put an "X" next to any of the above accounts that are exempt from TEFRA. *Exemptions:* <u>Trust, corporation, financial institution, individual retirement plan, government entitites etc.</u>
8. *Paper trail*—Briefly describe each of the seven steps in opening a typical new account.
   1. <u>Acquire and enter client information on form.</u>
   2. <u>Verify bank reference. Get necessary documents. Account executive signs application.</u>
   3. <u>Review and approval by branch manger.</u>
   4. <u>Get number from new accounts processor</u>
   5. <u>Transmit client's name/address to home office.</u>
   6. <u>Verify transmission information.</u>
   7. <u>Maintain client card file.</u>
9. What document must be sent to a client if he/she wants to open an option account?
   <u>Risk disclosure statement</u>
10. Jill Jones works for XYZ Brokerage Firm. What *must* she do before opening any account with ABC Brokerage Firm?
    <u>Get prior written permission from the designated officer of the firm.</u>
    (Duplicate copies of all confirmations and statements must be sent to that firm.)
11. Jill Jones is a registered account executive in New York. Her friend Mary Smith lives and works in New Jersey. Can Jill open an account for Mary?
    Yes_____ No <u>X</u>
12. Define:
    TEFRA—<u>Tax Equity and Responsibility Act</u>
    UGMA—<u>Uniform Gift to Minors Act</u>
    DVP—<u>Delivery vs. Payments</u>
    NOW—<u>Name and Address Over the Wire</u>

13. *Discretionary account*—Whenever an account is operated by another, either a full or a limited power of attorney is required.
14. *Custodian account*—The custodian must make only conservative (prudent) investments.
15. *Joint account*—Describe the difference between the two major types of joint accounts: JTWROS and tenants in common. The accounts differ in what happens when one of the owners dies. *Joint tenants with rights of survivorship*—The account becomes the full property of the survivor. *Tenants in common*—The decedent's portion of the account passes to the estate of the decedent and divided on a fifty-fifty basis unless otherwise stipulated in writing by both parties prior to death.

Correcting Account Information

These instructions are used to make changes on the New Account Application form. They are typical, and are used in many brokerage branch offices. However, the instructions used in your branch may be somewhat different. All corrections must be approved by the branch manager or the operations manager. You *may not*, for example, *change* the "name" or "registration." A typical account correction form would have the format shown in Figure 5-1.

Figure 5-1. Typical Account Correction Form.

ACCOUNT NUMBER
Client and Account Information
   Soc. Sec./Tax No.
   Geographical Location Code   Dividends — Hold/Pay
   Institutional ID No.   Zip Code
   Client Fund Choice   IRA
                                 Is client an employee?

PART ONE
Six lines for indicating changes in the
   Principal party (PP)
   or owner/portion of the account

You may be asked to change:
   The account executive number — needs branch
      manager approval
   Address of client, PP or IP — upon client
      instruction. Needs branch manager approval.
   Social Security number — upon client instruction.
      The sales assistant must get written confirmation,
      such as a W-9 form.

PART TWO
Six lines for adding, changing, or deleting another
   Interested Party (IP).
   When client wants duplicate copies of confirmations
      and statements sent to an Interested Party.
      There can be 1–7 IPs for an account.
      Send a separate wire transmission for each IP.
      Assign consecutive numbers, such as IP-1, IP-2.

PART THREE
Six lines for sending confirmations and statements to
   an Interested Party on a DVP account.
      See Lesson 6 for details on DVP accounts.

Before proceeding with this section, ask the operations manager for an account correction form and the exact procedures for your branch.

EXERCISE: 5:1
Account Correction Form

See your operations manager to get an Account Correction Form.

Instructions: In Lesson 4, Exercise 4.1, you completed a New Account Application Form for Harry Richards. It turns out that his last name is spelled "Richardson." Mr. Richardson's account number is 200-12345-1-2-012

1. Complete the Account Correction form indicating this change.

2. Before sending this correction over the wire, whose approval would need?

A week later you are informed that Harry Richardson wants to provide his lawyer and his accountant with copies of the confirmations and the monthly statement.

Mr. Richardson's lawyer's name and address is:

Mr. Tom Hall
324 East 36 Street
New York, NY 10001

Mr. Richardson's accountant's name and address is:

Mr. Paul Brown
Smith Accountants, Inc.
654 Main Street
Morristown, NJ 07960

3. How many forms would you fill out for these interested parties?

Fill out the Account Correction form(s).

THIS PAGE IS FOR A COPY OF
YOUR FIRM'S ACCOUNT CORRECTION FORM.

Institutional/Retail DVP New Account Application

This lesson includes instructions for opening an institutional/retail DVP (delivery versus payment) account. These accounts involve the use of agent banks and there are regulations governing the transactions. However, the exact procedure for establishing and maintaining accounts may vary from firm to firm.

Before proceeding with this section, ask the operations manger for an institutional/retail DVP new account application form and the exact procedures for your branch. Most brokerage branch offices have different internal requirements. Work with your operations manager on these requirements. Find out:

- The minimum size of the account (if any) per day

  _____

- and delivery standing instructions _____

  _____

  _____

A list of some of the symbols that will be used in the delivery process are:

- DVP—Delivery versus payment;
- RVP—Receive versus payment;
- ID—Institutional delivery;
- DTC—Depository trust company;
- BAS—Agent bank ID number.

THIS PAGE IS FOR A COPY OF YOUR FIRM'S
INSTITUTIONAL/RETAIL DVP/RVP APPLICATION FORM.

THIS PAGE IS FOR A COPY OF YOUR FIRM'S
FORM FOR THE ADDITION OF INTERESTED PARTIES.

Delivery Instructions

Deliveries will be made to banks in the state in which the client resides. The only exception is that deliveries will be made to any New York City bank no matter in which state the client resides. All delivery instructions must be full and accurate. This information obtained at the opening of the account will serve to guide all future trades clearing through the third party, such as the Depository Trust Company (DTC).

According to NYSE rules, the ease and efficiency of processing deliveries and receives dictates that all clients who qualify for the ID System must be on it.

Opening a Typical Institutional DVP Account

An institutional/retail DVP account is opened when a client chooses to transact business on a delivery versus payment (DVP) basis. Most sales assistants will help the account executive in opening such accounts; therefore, a thorough understanding of the details of these accounts will aid in the accurate processing of transactions.

When a client, either institutional (corporate, pension fund, bank-managed trust) or retail, chooses to trade on a *delivery versus payment* or *receive versus payment* (DVP/RVP) basis, the delivery of and payment for securities transactions are processed through an electronic *institutional delivery* (ID) service. This automated system facilitates the receiving and delivering of securities through a single entity, *the depository trust company* (DTC), to coordinate all of the settlement activity among brokers, institutions, custodian banks and other interested parties.

The account executive is responsible for obtaining:

- The agent bank ID number (BAS); and
- The client's account number at the agent bank.

If the client cannot give their customer number at this bank at the time the account is opened, the sales assistant should call the contact at the agent bank and obtain it.

There are no exceptions to branch procedure. All clients who wish to transact business on a delivery versus payment basis must complete the institutional/retail DVP new account application form.

Review and Approval

As with all new accounts the account executive must sign the form. The branch manager must indicate approval by also signing the form. The new accounts clerk must review the form as well, for completeness before assigning the appropriate account number.

Completing an
Institutional/Retail DVP Account Application Form

All previously discussed instructions for completing a new account application form apply to this form, as well. All necessary supporting documentation must be supplied. Following are the typical step-by-step instructions for completing the Institutional/ Retail DVP Accounts application form. Use the application form, and any special instructions you obtained from the operations manager to follow along with these instructions.

1. Account Number. The first line is for the account number, however, it cannot be filled in until the application form is completed, signed and approved along with the necessary documentation.

2. Social Security or Taxpayer Identification Number. Required under U.S. Treasury Department regulation 103.35. One or the other of these identification numbers MUST be entered. Exception: Foreign clients (non-U.S. citizens) who derive no income from the U.S.

3. Dividends. With DVP accounts the only option is to hold the dividends. This is indicated on the form.

4. DVP/RVP. DVP, delivery versus payment and/or RVP, receive versus payment. One or both instruction codes must be checked.

5. TEFRA. Tax Equity and Fiscal Responsibility Act. Check if the client is exempt. This fact must be confirmed with a completed W-9 TEFRA form.

6. Geographical Location. Fill in this area only if the client is not a U.S. resident. Necessary for correct dividend withholding tax.

7. Zip Code. Essential to transmission over the wire and efficient handling of confirmations and statements.

8. Legal Name and Mailing Address. Must be the correct name of the account. The mailing address should be the permanent residence. A post office box and/or a temporary address is unacceptable.

9. Home Telephone Number. Enter the number even if it is unlisted. Include area code.

10. Business Telephone Number. To maintain client contact. Initially it can be used to verify employment.

11. Date. The date the account is being opened.

Figure 6-1: Institutional/Retail DVP Account Application Form.

INSTITUTIONAL / RETAIL DVP ACCOUNT
ACCOUNT APPLICATION

1. Account number _____

   Client and account information _____

2. Social security /Federal tax ID number _____ 3. Dividends—hold _____

4. DVP/RVP _____ 5. TEFRA _____

6. Geographic location number _____

7. Zip code _____

8. Legal name and mailing address _____

   _____

   _____

9. Home telephone number _____

10. Business telephone number _____

11. Date _____

12. For additions and interested parties, use form _____.

13. Institutional ID number _____

14. Delivery instructions (include agent bank ID number and client account number at agent bank) _____

   _____

15. Receive instructions _____

   _____

16. Bank reference information _____

   _____

   _____

17. Accounts at other brokerage firms _____

   _____

18. Account executive registration _____

19. Discretionary authorization YES_____ NO_____ If yes, specify. _____

20. Initial transaction

   _____

21. Retail only _____

22. Approvals _____

   _____

12. For Addition of Interested Parties. See your operations manager to get a copy and instructions for the appropriate form when the client wants duplicate copies of confirmations and statements sent to an *interested party* (IP).

13. Institutional I.D. Number. This is also referred to as the customer's ID number. If the client is a money manager use his/her ID number.

14. Delivery Instructions. Six lines for information about the bank or institution that securities purchased will be delivered to against payment.

- *First Line*—If the account is on the Institutional Delivery System (ID), enter on this line "Account on ID System."
- *Second Line*—Enter the DTC number of the bank or institution. There are two parts to the Third Line:
- *Third Line, Top Part*—Enter the BAS number and the Customer number.

  BAS—Agent bank ID number. This number is recognized by the ID System and can be obtained in the DTC Book of Eligible Securities. It is sent to the branch office on a quarterly basis. Check with the operations manager for help with this section.

  CUST NUMBER—Client's account number at the agent bank. This is also referred to as the agent bank account number.

- *Third Line, Bottom Part*—This line is for accounts that are *not* on the institutional delivery system (ID).
- *Lines Four, Five, Six*—List the correct name of the account (A/C).

15. Receive Instructions. In most cases the receive and the deliver instructions will be the same. To indicate this, enter "same as above." If the receive instructions differ, use this area to completely enter the new instructions.

16. Bank Reference. Enter bank name, address, contact, phone. Indicate if this information has been verified. The name and phone number of the contact and department are most important. This gives the branch direct access should a problem arise.

17. Accounts at Other Brokerage Firms. Employees at any firm must give this information. And there must be written permission from their firm on file before the account may be opened.

18. Account Executive Registration. As with other new accounts, the account executive *must be* registered in the same state in which the client resides. If this is not the case, the account executive should *not* open the account. There should be an up-to-date listing of all branch office account executive registrations available to the new accounts clerk and/or the person responsible for assigning new accounts.

19. Discretionary Authorization. If someone other than the client—an agent—is authorized to transact business for the client, such as placing orders, check the "Yes" box and provide the full name and address of this individual. If this is not the case, check the "No" box.

20. Initial Transaction. If the account is going to trade immediately, details of the first transaction such as: buy/sell/other, number of shares, security, and dollar amount, must be entered.

21. The Retail Only. This section of the form should be completed for non-institutional or retail accounts as described in Lesson 4.

22. Approvals. The procedure for signing/approving the form is the same as in Lesson 4. In this section there is also a place for a suggested total dollar limit, approved dollar limit and the national credit department signature/approval. See the operations manager for the procedures on these credit items.

QUIZ 6:1
Institutional/Retail DVP/RVP Form

Instructions: Enter your response in the appropriate spaces.

1. What do each of these symbols represent?

RVP _____

DTC _____

BAS _____

2. If the client does not have the BAS, what book can the sales assistant use to find this information?

_____

3. When would the account number be entered on the form?

_____

4. For an RVP account, can the client choose to have the dividends sent to them? Yes_____   No_____

5. Can a client choose to transact business on a DVP basis without opening a DVP/RVP account? Yes_____   No_____

6. Employees of any brokerage firm need _____ before opening a DVP/RVP account.

7. If the client does not have their customer number, what would you do?

_____

QUIZ ANSWERS 6:1

Institutional/Retail DVP/RVP Form

1. What do each of these symbols represent?

   RVP—Receive versus Payment

   DTC—Depository Trust Company

   BAS—Agent Bank ID number

2. If the client does not have the BAS, what book can the sales assistant use to find this information?

   DTC Book of Eligible Securities

3. When would the account number be entered on the form?

   After it is signed/approved and the documents are in.

4. For an RVP account, can the client choose to have the dividends sent to them? Yes   No X

5. Can a client choose to transact business on a DVP basis without opening a DVP/RVP account? Yes   No   X

6. Employees of any brokerage firm need prior written permission before opening a DVP/RVP account.

7. If the client does not have their customer number, what would you do?

   Call the contact person at the agent bank.

Handling Various Types of Accounts

This lesson includes instructions for opening different types of accounts including:

- Option;
- Estate;
- Trust; and,
- Custodian.

All of these accounts are heavily regulated; however, the exact procedures and forms for the processing of transactions and the opening of new accounts will vary from firm to firm. It's the sales assistant's responsibility to check with the operations manager for the correct forms and procedures for that particular branch. This need to learn about your branch procedures is especially true for such internal matters as the filing of the *account card* and then purging inactive accounts.

Opening an Option Account

Before starting this section, obtain these necessary forms to open an option account in your branch.

Figure 7-1. Forms Required Prior to Opening an Option Account.

	Form No.	Date Obtained
Option Account Application Form	_____	_____
Risk Disclosure Statement	_____	_____
Option Strategy Guidelines	_____	_____
Option Suitability Form	_____	_____
Cash Account Option Agreement	_____	_____
Notice by Option/Compliance Dept.	_____	_____
Risks/Uses of Listed Options	_____	_____
Options on Debt Instruments	_____	_____
Commodity Option Agreement	_____	_____
_____	_____	_____
_____	_____	_____
_____	_____	_____

NOTES:

_____

_____

_____

_____

_____

_____

_____

_____

_____

_____

_____

_____

_____

_____

_____

_____

Typical Option Account Form Questions

Figure 7-2. Option Account Form Questions.

Date client received the Risk Disclosure Document _____

Equity options

Has client previously traded equity options?   Yes _____   No _____

 If yes, how long? As buyer _____ years   As seller _____ years

Do equity options suit client's objectives?   Yes _____   No _____

Is client aware of financial risks?   Yes _____   No _____

Equity option activity anticipated

____ Purchase calls   ____ Purchase puts   ____ Sell covered calls

____ Sell uncovered options   ____ Spreads

Debt options and other

Has client previously traded debt options?   Yes _____   No _____

 If yes, how long? As buyer _____ years   As seller _____ years

Do debt options suit client's objectives?   Yes _____   No _____

Is client aware of financial risks?   Yes _____   No _____

Debt activity anticipated

____ Purchase   ____ All other strategies   ____ Foreign currency

- Each question in the option section on the New Account form must be answered.
- You must provide the exact date the Risk Disclosure Statement was sent to the client including day, month, year.
- The account executive must be registered in the same state in which the client resides. Verify this registration with the New Accounts Clerk or branch manager's secretary.
- The account executive and the branch manager must sign and approve all new application forms.
- A separate Option Suitability form is required for each party in a joint account when they are not married.
- A separate Option Suitability form is required for each member of an investment club or partnership.
- No account should be opened with a Canadian address.

Option Suitability Form

Figure 7-3. Guidelines for Option Requirements.

Strategies/Investment Objectives	Annual Income	Net Worth Liquid	Net Worth Total
Purchase Options Speculative & Appreciation Risk	$150,000	$100,000	$200,000
Sell Covered Calls Income/Safety, Appreciation/Safety	$100,000	$100,000	$200,000
Spreads Speculative & Appreciation/Risk			
Sell Uncovered Options (Sell Straddles or Combo) Speculative & Appreciation/Risk	$250,000	$500,000	$100,000
Purchase Puts, Sell Covered Calls Only for IRA, Keogh, Custodian Income/Safety & Appreciation/ Safety	$100,000	$100,000	$200,000
Debt Options, Foreign Currency, All Strategies Speculative, Appreciation/Risk	$250,000	$500,000	$100,000

The following information must always be completed on an Option Suitability form.

1. Employer's name, client's occupation;

2. Annual income;

3. Liquid net worth;

4. Total net worth;

5. Investment objectives;

6. Investment experience;

7. Date client received Risk Disclosure Statement;

8. Marital status; and

9. Age, Number of dependents.

Estate, Trust, and Custodian Accounts

Estate Accounts
The following is a list of the correct information required when opening a new estate account.

1. The correct account title format for opening new estate accounts is:

Mr. Harry Jones, Exec. (admin., etc.)
Estate of James Jones

2. When a client dies, the procedure to follow is:

- not to open a new account;
- mark the account "deceased" until the estate documentation is received; and
- when the estate documentation is received at the branch office, change the existing account to read:

> Paul Thomas Exec.
> Estate of Robert Thomas

3. The procedure to follow when the executor of the estate of a deceased client requests a transfer of securities to the beneficiary is:

- Change the name of the account to read:

> Peter Brown, Exec.
> Estate of John Brown

when the estate documentation and state tax waivers are received at the branch office.

- Open a new account in the name of the beneficiary with all of the proper documentation and journals.

4. Trustees are appointed after the "estate" has been settled. After this has occurred the correct title format is:

> Sally White Trs.
> U/W/O Peggy White

5. The name of the beneficiary should not be included in the title of "estate" accounts.

> *Exception:* In testamentary trusts, names of beneficiaries may be included in the title. This is optional.

> (Required) Charles Allen Trs.
> (Required) U/W/O Joan Allen
> (Optional) FBO Laura Allen

6. The date of the will is not to be included in the title of "estate" accounts and testamentary trusts.

7. When both parties of a joint account are deceased, an "estate" account should be opened for the tenant who dies last. Use this title format:

> William Dan, Exec.
> Estate of Shirley Dan

8. In the case of a joint account with rights of survivorship (WROS), the surviving tenant is entitled to 100 percent of the assets of the account. Tax waivers, in states where issued, are required for 100 percent of the account value. Enter "Decd" after the decedent's name. Do not delete the name of the deceased and the survivor's name remains as it is.

The title should be changed as follows:

Jean Clair Decd.
Richard Clair

A new account must be opened in the individual name of the survivor. Journals or the securities from the existing joint account may be delivered to the survivor.

NOTES:

_____

_____

_____

_____

_____

_____

Opening Trust Accounts

1. Living (inter vivos) trust accounts—The correct title for this account is in this order:

a. Name of trustee   i.e., Alice Mack Trs.
b. Date of trust agreement   U/A 3-6-82
c. FBO (for benefit of)   FBO Jody Mack
beneficiary name

Below is an INCORRECT title of a living trust account.

a. Name of living trust   i.e., The Alice Mack Trust
b. Date of trust agreement   Dated 3-6-82
c. Name of trustee   Alice Mack Trs.

In this example, the name of the beneficiary is not clear.

2. ERISA accounts (pension, profit-sharing, retirement, and so on)—The correct title for this account is in this order:

a. Name of corporation   i.e., Allied Corp.
b. Type of trust   Employees Pension Plan & Trust DTD
c. Date of trust   Dated 2-4-84

The firm must have a copy of the trust on file. However, it is not necessary to have a copy of the plan unless the plan and trust are part of the same document.

NOTES:

_____

_____

_____

_____

_____

Handling Wills, Inter Vivos Trusts (Trustee), and ERISA Accounts

1. The procedure for handling wills is as follows:

a. Verify that the will is a true copy. That means that it must be subscribed by the decedent and witnessed by two witnesses, or that it has been certified by the court and an attorney.

b. Check the investment powers of the fiduciary. Look for key words such as "invest, reinvest, purchase or acquire securities, stocks, bonds" and so on.

c. Liquidation only—No will is required.

d. Fiduciary/administrator—No will is required if the fiduciary has been appointed as the administrator.

e. California estates—No will is required. A court order of distribution or sale takes the place of a will.

Exception: No court order is required if appointment of the fiduciary allows the fiduciary to administer the estate without court approval.

f. Primary function of estates—Because estates are intended to be liquidated or distributed, no trades are allowed unless express powers are there.

2. The procedure for handling inter vivos trusts (or trustees) is as follows:

a. Verify that the following information coincides with the account title:

Name of trustee(s) (usually found on Page One)

Effective date of trust (usually found on Page One)

Beneficiary and grantor.

b. Check investment powers of the trustee(s):

Look for key words such as "invest and reinvest, purchase or acquire securities, stocks, bonds" and so on. For certain transactions such as trade options and/or commodities, you must check with the operations manager for the specific language that is required.

c. Check signatures. All trust agreements must be signed by the trustee. Verify this requirement.

3. The procedure for handling ERISA and pension, profit-sharing, or retirement trusts is as follows:

a. Verify that the following information coincides with the account title:

Name of trust (usually found on Page One)

Effective date of trust (usually found on Page One)

Name of trustee(s) (usually found on Page One)

b. Check investment powers of the trustee(s). Look for key words such as "invest and reinvest, purchase or acquire securities, bonds," and so on.

c. Verify all signatures. All trust agreements must be signed by the trustee.

d. The firm must have a copy of the trust on file. However, it is not necessary to have a copy of the plan unless the plan is part of the same instrument.

e. Check restrictions. ERISA trusts may not be opened to transact margin, short selling or uncovered-option writing.

NOTES:

_____

_____

_____

_____

_____

_____

Handling Guardian, Committee, and Conservator Accounts

1. By court appointments, the court determines whether the account is to be as guardian, committee or conservator. Only use these designations when the client has provided the branch with a recently-dated court appointment.

2. The correct title for guardian, committee, or conservator accounts is in this order:

a. Name of fiduciary	i.e., Tom Scott	
b. Proper fiduciary title	Guardian	
c. Name of ward	for Jane Scott	

Handling Custodian Accounts

1. The correct title for custodian accounts are in this order:

a. Name of custodian	i.e., Joe Judd	
b. Name of minor	Jimmy Judd	
c. State law under which the gift was originally made	U/T/NY/U/G to Minors Act	

Law permits choice of state of donor's or minor's residence.

2. A gift can be made to only one minor and there is only one minor allowed per account.

3. Only one person may be custodian of the same custodial property and there is only one custodian per account.

4. The procedure to follow when the minor attains the age of majority:

- Should the former minor elect to stay with the firm, a new account must be opened in his/her name. Verify the age by requesting a certified copy of the birth certificate.
- Should the former minor want the security issued in registered form, transfer instructions must be given to the branch back office. Verify the age by requesting a certified copy of the birth certificate.

Summary

A custodian account is established when a gift is made under the Unified Gift to Minors Act. Guardians, Committees and Conservators are established by the court to handle the affairs of someone the court has determined is incapable of handling their own affairs. All trust transactions are regulated by the trust instrument or agreement. See your branch manager for any additional details you may need concerning your firm's policies on establishing these new accounts.

NOTES:

_____

_____

_____

_____

_____

_____

The 3×5 New Account Card

A good idea, used by many firms today, is the 3×5 account card. Each account executive should have a 3×5 client/account card on each account he/she is responsible for handling. It can be filed by account number or client name. Many firms supply account executives with two sets of cards: one in alphabetical order and the other in client number order. (See Figure 7-4 for an example of a new account card.)

The 3×5 new account cards are generated when an account is opened. Use one card for the account executive and one card for the back office.

When any changes are made in the account, such as an address change, a document received, a change of dividend instructions, or any other changes, only the most recent card must be on file. A "date of change" must be noted on each card, and all old cards must be destroyed immediately and replaced by the new card.

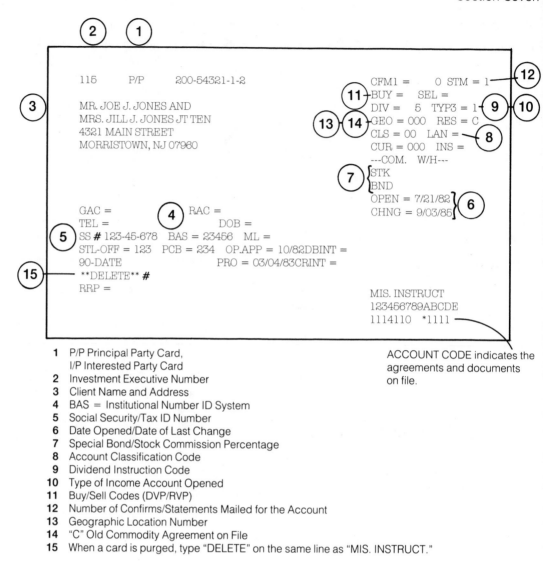

1 P/P Principal Party Card,
   I/P Interested Party Card
2 Investment Executive Number
3 Client Name and Address
4 BAS = Institutional Number ID System
5 Social Security/Tax ID Number
6 Date Opened/Date of Last Change
7 Special Bond/Stock Commission Percentage
8 Account Classification Code
9 Dividend Instruction Code
10 Type of Income Account Opened
11 Buy/Sell Codes (DVP/RVP)
12 Number of Confirms/Statements Mailed for the Account
13 Geographic Location Number
14 "C" Old Commodity Agreement on File
15 When a card is purged, type "DELETE" on the same line as "MIS. INSTRUCT."

Figure 7-4. The 3×5 New Account Card.

NOTES:

Purging Inactive Accounts

Each brokerage firm has its own policy for purging an account that shows no activity and has no positions and/or balances. Check with your operations manager for the time allowed before an account is purged. Be sure to enter how many years the file has been inactive.

A typical purge policy is to purge the account if it is inactive for a period of three years, or if there was no activity for one year after it was opened. These accounts are systematically purged after every month-end statement.

When an account is purged, the word "delete" and the effective date will be entered on the 3×5 account card, as shown in Figure 7-5. The name and address will be deleted from the new account file. Two new 3×5 cards will be sent to the branch office. Then one 3×5 card will be given to the account executive advising him/her that the account is closed and not to be used again.

If a client whose account has been closed decides to do business with the firm again, *under no circumstances is the same account number to be used again.* This client is to be treated as if he/she is a new account and has not done business with the firm before. The correct procedure for such a client is:

- Complete a new New Account Application form;
- Have the form signed by the account executive and approved by the branch manager;
- Obtain all new supporting documentation; and
- Have a new account number assigned.

Figure 7-5. Purging Inactive Accounts.

```
115      P/P       200-54321-1-2              CFM1 =      0 STM = 1
                                              BUY =    SEL =
MR. JOE J. JONES AND                          DIV =    5  TYP3 = 1
MRS. JILL J. JONES JT TEN                     GEO = 000  RES = C
4321 MAIN STREET                              CLS = 00  LAN =
MORRISTOWN, NJ 07960                          CUR = 000  INS =
                                              ---COM.  W/H---
                                              STK
                                              BND
                                              OPEN = 7/21/82
GAC =             RAC =                        CHNG = 9/03/84
TEL =                   DOB =
SS # 123-45-678  BAS = 23456   ML =
STL-OFF = 123  PCB = 234  OP.APP = 10/82DBINT =
90-DATE                 PRO = 03/04/83CRINT =

RRP =                                         MIS. INSTRUCT
                                              123456789ABCDE
                                              1114110  *1111
```

QUIZ 7:1

Handling Various Types of Accounts

Instructions: Enter your response in the appropriate spaces.

1. What three economic factors are most important in judging a client's suitability for opening an option account?

   _____

   _____

   _____

2. Which document must the client get when opening an option account?

   _____

3. Investment clubs and partnerships require a _____

   Option Suitability on _____ _____.

4. What's the correct title format for new estate accounts?

   _____

   _____

5. Define WROS.

   _____

   _____

   _____

6. What's the correct title format for living trust accounts?

   _____

   _____

7. Name three types of ERISA accounts.

   _____

   _____

   _____

8. Do California estates require a will? Yes_____ No_____

9. What are the key words you look for to define the investment powers of a trustee?

   _____

   _____

10. Decisions about guardians, committees and conservators

    are made by _____.

11. Custodian accounts are usually set up to regulate gifts given under what law?

    _____

12. Give four reasons to generate a new 3×5 new account card.

_____

_____

_____

_____

13. What would be typed on the 3×5 new account card to indicate a purged account?

_____

14. Accounts are usually purged when there is _____
for a specific period of time.

NOTES:

QUIZ ANSWERS 7:1

Handling Various Types of Accounts

1. What three economic factors are most important in judging a client's suitability for opening an option account?
   Annual Income
   Liquid Net Worth
   Total Net Worth

2. Which document must the client get when opening an option account?
   Risk Disclosure Document

3. Investment clubs and partnerships require a separate Option Suitability on each member.

4. What's the correct title format for new estate accounts?
   Mr. Joseph Brown, Exec.
   Estate of Mary Brown

5. Define WROS.
   With Rights of Survivorship

6. What's the correct title format for living trust accounts?
   Joe Brown
   U/A 8-12-84
   FBO Jimmy Brown

7. Name three types of ERISA accounts.
   Pension
   Profit Sharing
   Retirement

8. Do California estates require a will? Yes   No X

9. What are the key words you look for to define the investment powers of a trustee?
   Invest and reinvest
   Purchase or acquire securities, stocks, bonds, etc.

10. Decisions about guardians, committees and conservators are made by the court.

11. Custodian accounts are usually set up to regulate gifts given under what law?
    Unified Gift to Minors Act

12. Give four reasons to generate a new 3×5 new account card.
    An account is opened
    Change of address
    Document received
    Dividend instruction change

13. What would be typed on the 3×5 new account card to indicate a purged account?
    DELETE

14. Accounts are usually purged when there is no activity for a specific period of time.

New Account Procedures: How to Obtain Documents

Completing the new account application form is of primary importance in opening any new account. Vital to this process is having the client supply all of the necessary documentation. One of the major responsibilities of the sales assistant is obtaining these documents from the client. Remember, however, that the adequacy of the new account documentation is a legal decision. You will often be instructed by counsel to obtain additional information and/or documentation.

Procedures vary from branch to branch, and from firm to firm. The sales assistant must check with the operations manager to find out exactly what the approved procedures are for their particular branch.

This section will review the document requirements of:

- margin accounts;
- trust accounts;
- ERISA accounts;
- commodity accounts;
- investment club accounts;
- discretionary accounts;
- estate accounts; and
- option accounts.

Guidelines for Obtaining Documents

When the client opens an account in the office:

- Make every effort to get the client to sign the documents immediately after the new account form is completed.
- If only one party to a joint account is present, give him/her the documents and an addressed, postage-paid envelope with a request for obtaining the other signature and mailing the documents back.
- Each sales assistant is responsible for obtaining all the necessary documents for each different account. The new accounts clerk or operations manager can help but it's really up to you. If the documents have not been received in ten days, follow up by calling the client.

When the client opens an account over the phone:

- The sales assistant should mail all of the documents to the client with an addressed, postage-paid envelope.

Branch Procedures

- In some branches it is the responsibility of the new accounts clerk to handle the documentation. Check with your operations manager.
- All documents should be inspected by you for completeness and signatures. When properly signed, make sure the entire account number is on the documents and give them to the new accounts clerk to be mailed back to the home office.

Customer Agreement (Margin)
The customer agreement covers all types of accounts including cash, margin and option. Always be certain that the following are correct on the documents:

- Two signatures are necessary on this customer agreement for each owner.
- When a margin trade is transacted and/or a debit is carried into the account the margin provisions in the agreement become operative.
- No client-generated alterations are allowed. For example, if the client whites out any portion of the agreement, it must be rejected.
- If a registration error is discovered within five days, the title may be changed. More than five days, and a new account must be opened with the correct ownership or registration.
- If more than two clients are joint owners of the account (tenants in common), all must sign and each percentage of ownership should be indicated.

NOTE:

_____

_____

_____

_____

_____

Trust Accounts

A complete copy of the trust agreement must be on file. For trading on margin or trading options or commodities, specific permission must be granted in the agreement. The account title must include (in this order):

Name of the Trustee (except corporate accounts)
Name of Trust
Date of Trust

NOTE:

_____

_____

_____

_____

_____

ERISA Accounts (Employee Retirement Income Security Act)

For ERISA accounts to trade on margin or to trade options or commodities, approval is needed from the firm's compliance department.

NOTE:

_____

_____

_____

_____

_____

Defined Benefit/Profit-sharing Plans

The branch does not need either a copy of the plan itself or a copy of the trust that operates the plan.

NOTE:

_____

_____

_____

_____

_____

Commodity Accounts

The Risk Disclosure Statement must remain with the client. If it comes back with the signed agreement, you must send it back to the client.

NOTE:

_____

_____

_____

_____

_____

Investment Club Accounts

These accounts must include the names, addresses and social security numbers of all members of the investment club. For trading options, the Compliance Department must approve a suitability form for each member.

NOTE:

_____

_____

_____

_____

_____

Discretionary Accounts

Policy on these accounts varies from firm to firm. _Limited discretion_ means that a third party cannot take money or securities out of the account; the third party can only trade the account. A typical discretionary account policy might be as follows:

- _Security Account Limited Discretionary Authorization_—An employee of the firm is given trading authorization.
- _Security Account Third Party Limited Discretionary Authorization_—A person other than an employee of the firm has trading authorization.
- _Commodity Account Limited Discretionary Authorization_—An employee of the firm has trading authorization over a commodity account.
- _Commodity Account Third Party Limited Discretionary Authorization_—A person other than an employee of the firm has trading authorization over a commodity account.

The firm has documents to be completed for each of these discretionary accounts and an information form. The following are important points to remember when filing these documents:

- The agent named must be an individual, not a company.
- The client must sign the form. For joint accounts, both clients must sign.
- The client's signature must be notarized. This person cannot be the agent.
- the agent must sign the form. Then the branch manager signs and approves it.
- Make copies of all documents for the branch.
- Forward all original documents to the compliance department.
- The compliance department must review the documents. If it approves, they will notify the branch manager.
- *No discretionary transactions are to be allowed without prior Compliance Department approval.*
- Finally, the account executive is given a copy of the notice.

NOTE:

_____

_____

_____

_____

_____

Estate Accounts

For the client to prove that he/she is the court-appointed executor or administrator of an estate account, a certified copy of *Letters Testamentary,* dated within 60 days, must be provided to the branch.

All securities that the client wants to be deposited in an estate account and the documents needed to *clear* them must come in together. Check with the cashier for the exact documents. The reason for this procedure is that insurance will not cover securities kept in a branch overnight.

NOTE:

_____

_____

_____

_____

_____

Option Accounts

It is the sales assistant's responsibility to provide the client with the customer agreement and risk disclosure statement. Follow up to insure prompt return of the customer agreement. This is essential to opening the account.

The client has fifteen (15) days after the approval of the account to sign and return the customer agreement. Without this agreement, the client will be limited to closing transactions only.

Clients trading equity options and/or debt options must be sent risk disclosure statements covering:

- listed options;
- listed options on stock indices; and
- listed options on foreign currencies.

NOTE:

_____

_____

_____

_____

_____

_____

_____

Documentation Requirements

All new accounts require a:

- New Account Form, and
- either a Customer Agreement or Commodity Customer Agreement.

In addition, depending on the type of transactions expected, an account may also require a:

- Cash account agreement.
- Margin account agreement.
- Option account agreement.
- Commodity account agreement.

Table 8-1 lists other forms that may be necessary, depending on the type of account. To the right in this table is a series of fill-in lines. Use these lines to insert your firm's names or numbers for the forms. You will also want to gather these forms either before, or as you use them. Work with the operations manager to identify these forms' names/numbers and to obtain copies of all of them, or at least of the ones you will likely to be using first.

Table 8-1. Forms Needed for Various Types of Accounts.

Individual Accounts, Joint Accounts (WROS or as Tenants in Common)
New account form
  (cash, margin, option, or commodities)   # _____

Customers agreement
  (cash, margin, or options)   # _____

Commodity customers agreement   # _____

Community Property Account
Community property agreement
  (cash, margin, options, commodities)   # _____

Corporation Account
Corporate agreement (cash)   # _____

Corporate agreement (margin options)   # _____

Corporate agreement (commodity) and
  by laws/articles of incorporation   # _____

Partnership Account
Co-partnership agreement
  (cash, margin, options, commodities)   # _____

Commodities client's partnership
  certificate   # _____

Investment Club
Investment club agreement (cash)   # _____

Investment club agreement
  (margin, options)   # _____

Sole Proprietorship
Certificate of sole proprietorship
  (cash, margin, options, commodities)   # _____

Unincorporated Association
Articles of association, and resolution
  naming authorized officer(s)
  (cash, margin, options, commodities)   # _____

Custodian Account (UGTMA), Uniform Gifts/Transfers to Minors Act)
Transactions prohibited by UGTMA
  (margin, commodities)   # _____

Cash-type options only   # _____

Usufruct Account
New account form (cash, margin, options) # _____

Customers agreement (cash, margin,
  options)   # _____

Educational Institution
Resolution naming authorized officer(s)
(cash, margin, options, commodities) # _____

Approval from legal department
(for commodities) # _____

Nonprivate/Charitable Organization
Articles of association and resolution
naming authorized officer(s)
(cash, margin, options, commodities) # _____

Needs approval from legal department
(for commodities) # _____

Recognized Religious Group
Corporate agreement (cash) # _____

Corporate agreement (margin, options) # _____

Corporate agreement (commodity)
and by laws/articles of incorporation.
Needs approval from legal department # _____

Numbered Account
Numbered account letter
(cash, margin, options, commodities) # _____

Needs approval from legal department
(for commodities) # _____

Mutual Fund
Requires prior approval from
commodity legal # _____

Hedge Fund
Co-partnership agreement and clients
partnership certificate
(cash, margin, options, commodities) # _____

Requires prior approval from
commodity legal # _____

Banking Institution
Resolution naming authorized officer(s)
(cash) # _____

Specific state laws/statutes
(margin, options) # _____

Corporate agreement (commodity).
By laws/articles of incorporation
and hedge letter # _____

Insurance Company
Resolution naming authorized officer(s)
(cash) # _____

Specific state laws (statutes)
(margin, options) # _____

Corporate agreement (commodity) and
   articles of association and
   specific state laws (statutes)   # _____

Broker/Dealer
New account form (cash, margin, options) # _____

Customers agreement (cash, margin,
   options)   # _____

Corporate agreement (commodity) and
   articles of association and specific
   state laws (statutes) and special
   requirements for investment clubs   # _____

Listed Company
Resolution naming authorized officer(s)
   (cash, margin, options, commodities)   # _____

Omnibus Account
Omnibus agreement ASEF Form 119
   (cash, margin, options)   # _____

Requires prior approval from legal
   department (for commodities)   # _____

Government Agency
Resolution naming authorized officer(s)
   (cash, margin, options, commodities)   # _____

Specific state laws (statutes)
   (margin, options)   # _____

Corporate agreement (commodity) and
   hedge letter, needs approval from
   legal department   # _____

ERISA Account
Trust agreement (ERISA)
   (cash, margin, commodities)   # _____

Not suitable (margin)   # _____

Cash-type only, needs specific language
   (options)   # _____

Needs approval from legal department
   (commodity)   # _____

IRA/Keogh
Adoption agreement (ERISA) and
   Prototype trust (ERISA) (Cash, options)   # _____

Margin is not suitable   # _____

Needs specific language and letter of
   commitment (for options trading)   # _____

Needs approval from legal department
   (for commodities)   # _____

Living Trust (Inter vivos)
   Trust agreement (inter vivos)
      (cash, margin, options, commodities)   # _____

   Needs specific language for margin,
      options, commodities   # _____

   Needs approval from legal department
      for commodities   # _____

Testamentary Trust (U/W/O)
   Court appointment of fiduciary
      (cash, margin, options, commodities)   # _____

   Needs specific language and procedure
      (for margin, options, commodities)   # _____

   Needs approval from legal department
      (for commodities)   # _____

Estate Account (Testate)
   Court appointment of fiduciary
      (cash, margin, options, commodities)   # _____

   Copy of will, needs specific language and
      special procedure for margin,
      options, commodities   # _____

   Needs approval from legal department
      for commodities   # _____

Estate Account (Intestate)
   Court appointment of fiduciary
      (cash, options)
   Cash-type options only   # _____

   Not suitable for margin or commodity   # _____

Life Tenant (U/W/O)
   Copy of will
      (cash, margin, options, commodities)   # _____

   Needs specific language and special
      procedures (margin, options,
      commodities)   # _____

   Needs approval from legal department
      for commodities   # _____

Guardianship Account and Conservatorship Account and Committee
   Court appointment of fiduciary
      (cash, options)   # _____

   Cash-type options only   # _____

   Not suitable (for margin or commodities)   # _____

Commodity Pool
    Needs special procedure for cash,
        margin, options, commodities   # _____

Other Documents that might be required:
    Check with your operations manager for in-structions in the specific use of the following documents.

    Joint Agreement   # _____

    Cash Option Agreement   # _____

    Commodity Hedge Agreement   # _____

    Discretionary Account Information Form   # _____

    Security Account Limited Discretionary
        Form   # _____

    Security Account Third-party Limited
        Discretionary Authorization Form   # _____

    Commodity Account Limited Discretionary
        Authorization Form   # _____

    Commodity Account Third-party Limited
        Discretionary Authorization Form   # _____

    Guaranty of Account   # _____

    Multiple Account Form   # _____

    Affidavit of Domicile   # _____

    Commodity Option Agreement   # _____

    General Power of Attorney   # _____

    Joint Venture Agreement   # _____

    Blanket Letter   # _____

    Small Estate Affidavit   # _____

    Letter of Consent   # _____

    Birth Certificates   # _____

    Amendment to Trust   # _____

    Death Certificate   # _____

NOTE:

_____

_____

_____

_____

_____

QUIZ 8:1
New Account Documentation

Instructions: Enter your response in the appropriate spaces.

1. Which two documents are necessary for all accounts?

_____

_____

2. Define ERISA.

_____

_____

3. List three types of discretionary accounts.

_____

_____

_____

4. List the three risk disclosure statements sent to the client.

_____

_____

_____

5. Should the client return the risk disclosure statement with the customer agreement, what must the sales assistant do?

_____

6. If a registration error is discovered after five days, what must be done?

_____

_____

7. With an educational institution, who must approve commodity trading?

_____

8. With a custodian account, what two types of transactions are prohibited by the UGMA?

_____

_____

9. With a corporation account, what documents are needed

for *cash* transactions? _____

for *margin* transactions? _____

for *commodity* transactions? _____

and which business document? _____

10. With a testamentary trust (U/W/O), what is necessary for all transactions?

_____

11. With an estate account (intestate) what kind of option trading is allowed?

_____

12. With trust accounts, what must appear in the trust agreement to trade on margin or trade options?

_____

13. With an insurance company account, what must be researched to trade on margin or trade options?

_____

14. For an ERISA account, is trading on margin allowed?

_____

NOTES

_____
_____
_____
_____
_____
_____
_____
_____
_____
_____
_____
_____
_____
_____
_____
_____
_____
_____
_____
_____
_____
_____
_____
_____
_____
_____
_____
_____

QUIZ ANSWERS 8:1

New Account Documentation

1. Which two documents are necessary for all accounts?
   New Account Form
   Customers Agreement

2. Define ERISA.
   Employee Retirement Income Security Act

3. List three types of discretionary accounts.
   Security Account Limited Discretionary Authorization
   Security Account 3rd Party Limited Discretionary Authorization
   Commodity Account Limited Discretionary Authorization

4. List the three risk disclosure statements sent to the client:
   Listed Options
   Listed Options on Stock Indices
   Listed Options on Foreign Currencies

5. Should the client return the risk disclosure statement with the customer agreement, what must the sales assistant do?
   Send the Risk Disclosure Statement back to client.

6. If a registration error is discovered after five days, what must be done?
   Open a new account with the correct ownership or registration.

7. With an educational institution, who must approve commodity trading?
   The firm's legal department

8. With a custodian account, what two types of transactions are prohibited by the UGMA?
   Trade on margin
   Commodity trading

9. With a corporation account, what documents are needed
   for *cash* transactions? Corporate Agreement (Cash)
   for *margin* transactions? Corporate Agreement (Margin)
   for *commodity* transactions? Corporate Agreement (Commodity)
   and which business document? Articles of Incorporation

10. With a testamentary trust (U/W/O), what is necessary for all transactions?
    Court appointment of a fiduciary

11. With an estate account (intestate) what kind of option trading is allowed?
    Cash-type only

12. With trust accounts, what must appear in the trust agreement to trade on margin or trade options?
    Specific language allowing such trades

13. With an insurance company account, what must be researched to trade on margin or trade options?
    Specific state laws (statutes)

14. For an ERISA account, is trading on margin allowed.
    No

Transfers of Accounts

As a sales assistant you will be involved in the transfer of accounts. For instance, if a client or his/her account executive relocates, the client may request that his/her account be transferred from one branch office to another. As usual, accuracy and efficiency on the part of the sales assistant are paramount in effecting a smooth transfer, as well as maintaining good client relations.

Accounts may be transferred any one of these three ways:

1. from one branch office to another within the same firm,

2. from a competitive firm to your branch, and/or

3. from your branch to a competitive firm.

In every case, however, an account cannot be transferred without:

- the approval of the branch managers of both offices involved; and

- the completion of a New Account Application by the account executive receiving the account.

The specifics of account transfers vary markedly from firm to firm. Therefore *it is necessary that you consult the person responsible for the new accounts function in your branch and your account executive to familiarize yourself with the proper transfer pro-*

cedures. The exercise sheets at the end of this lesson are designed to help you collect the necessary information.

Please complete the brief quiz on the following page before proceeding to the exercise sheets.

QUIZ 9:1
Transfers of Accounts

For each item write the appropriate responses in the spaces provided.

1. List the three ways in which an account may be transferred:

a. _____

b. _____

c. _____

2. List the two requirements for any type of account transfer:

a. _____

b. _____

QUIZ ANSWERS 9:1

Transfers of Accounts

1. List the three ways in which an account may be transferred:

   a. From one branch to another within the same firm.

   b. From a competitive firm to your branch.

   c. From your branch to a competitive firm.

2. List the two requirements for any type of account transfer:

   a. The approval of the branch managers of both offices involved.

   b. The completion of a New Account Application by the account executive receiving the account.

EXERCISE 9:1
Transfers of Accounts

From Branch to Branch

See the person responsible for the new accounts function in your branch (see your organizational chart from Exercise 1:1 for his/her name, if necessary) and your account executive for answers to the following account transfer procedure questions. Enter the appropriate information in the space provided.

What forms are used to transfer accounts from branch to branch?

(Collect all forms and *enter their names and form numbers in the space below* before proceeding. You will need this information when reordering forms.)

_____   _____

_____   _____

_____   _____

What is the procedure for transferring accounts from branch to branch?

1. _____
2. _____
3. _____
4. _____
5. _____
6. _____
7. _____
8. _____
9. _____
10. _____

If the account title will change (for example, "Mr. John Jones" to "Mr. John Jones, Jr."), what must be done to put the account in a new name during transfer?

_____

_____

_____

EXERCISE 9:2
Transfers of Accounts

From Competitive Firm to Your Branch

See the person responsible for the new accounts function in your branch and your account executive for answers to the following account transfer procedure questions. Enter the appropriate information in the space provided.

What forms are used to transfer accounts from competitive firms to your branch?

(Collect all forms and *enter their names and form numbers in the space below* before proceeding. You will need this information when reordering forms.)

_____ _____

_____ _____

_____ _____

What is the procedure for transferring accounts from competitive firms to your branch?

1. _____

2. _____

3. _____

4. _____

5. _____

6. _____

7. _____

8. _____

9. _____

10. _____

How is a partial transfer handled?

_____

_____

_____

EXERCISE 9:3
Transfers of Accounts

From Your Branch to a Competitive Firm

See the person responsible for the new accounts function in your branch and your account executive for answers to the following account transfer procedure questions. Enter the appropriate information in the space provided.

What forms are used to transfer accounts from your branch to competitive firms?

(Collect all forms and *enter their names and form numbers in the space below* before proceeding. You will need this information when reordering forms.)

_____ _____

_____ _____

_____ _____

What is the procedure for transferring accounts from your branch to competitive firms?

1. _____
2. _____
3. _____
4. _____
5. _____
6. _____
7. _____
8. _____
9. _____
10. _____

NOTES:

Nonsecurities Products

Nonsecurities products are investment vehicles such as insurance annuities, tax shelters, IRAs, and Keogh accounts. Because they vary considerably from firm to firm and even from branch to branch, this lesson will consist of a series of exercises aimed at:

- identifying your branch's nonsecurities products;
- acquiring and reviewing the documentation for each product (promotional brochures and processing forms);
- learning how each product is processed; and
- learning how to carry out your duties relative to each product.

  You will need the assistance of your branch operations manager in completing the following exercises.

EXERCISE 10:1
Nonsecurities Products

Your Branch's Nonsecurities Products

Ask your operations manager for assistance in completing this exercise. (Be sure to record all pertinent information in the space provided.)

What are the names of the off-the-board products sold in our branch?

1. _____
2. _____
3. _____
4. _____
5. _____
6. _____
7. _____
8. _____
9. _____
10. _____
11. _____
12. _____

Acquire and review the documentation for each product (promotional literature and processing forms). Be sure to keep them in this book for future reference.

EXERCISE 10:2
Nonsecurities Products

<hr>

Using the worksheets provided on the following pages along with the documentation acquired in Exercise 10:1, ask your operations manager to provide you with the following information for each product:

- the steps by which the product is processed;
- your duties relative to the processing of each product, including the interpretation of all forms and how they are filled out.

Be sure to take clear, comprehensive notes for future reference.

WORKSHEET

Product name _____

Steps for Processing

1. _____
2. _____
3. _____
4. _____
5. _____
6. _____
7. _____
8. _____
9. _____
10. _____

Your Duties

1. _____
2. _____
3. _____
4. _____
5. _____
6. _____
7. _____
8. _____
9. _____
10. _____

Notes on forms (interpreting each form's contents and filling it out).

NOTES:

Publications

Most investment decisions are based on hard, factual data about companies and their markets, as well as the economy. Naturally, such information is vital for account executives and clients alike. But where do they get the information? The sources are varied, ranging from personal contacts within companies or in-house corporate economists to specialized publications. In this lesson, the focus will be on publications and your role relative to their use as a decision-making aid. Without publications, it would be very difficult for your account executive to select the best product(s) for each client's needs, much less convince the client to buy the product(s).

As sales assistant you need to be able to quickly assist your account executive and clients in getting various pieces of information. In doing so, you will be using both internal and outside publications. Let's now take a look at commonly used outside publications and how they are used.

Outside Publications

Standard and Poor's Reports (S&P Sheets)

Standard and Poor's Reports are published for individual companies traded in these marketplaces:

- the New York Stock Exchange (NYSE);
- the American Stock Exchange (AMEX); and
- the over-the-counter (OTC) market.

Figure 11-1. A Sample Page from a Standard & Poor's Report.

Georgia-Pacific

1006

NYSE Symbol GP   Put & Call Options on Phil

Price	Range	P-E Ratio	Dividend	Yield	S&P Ranking
Feb. 2'82 18½	1981-2 32⅜-17¼	12	1.20	6.5%	A–

Summary

The largest domestic producer of softwood plywood, this leading forest products company also has major interests in the chemical and gypsum fields. While earnings will continue to be influenced by changes in housing activity, long-term prospects are enhanced by GP's strong position in primary markets and its large capital program. On September, 1981 an appeals court in New Orleans upheld a 1978 jury verdict which found GP and two other firms guilty of fixing plywood prices.

Current Outlook

Earnings for 1982 should post some recovery from the depressed $1.51 a share of 1981.

Dividends should remain at $0.30 quarterly.

Aided by recent capacity additions and projected firming trends in major markets during the second half, sales for 1982 are likely to show further progress. Despite rising costs, profitability should benefit from extensive cost controls and improved efficiency.

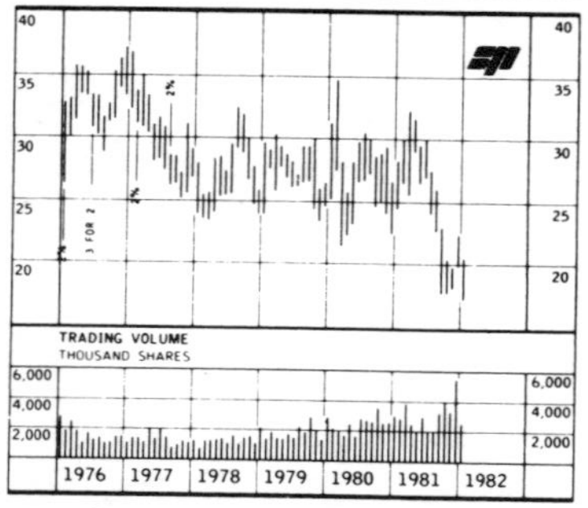

Sales (Million $)

Quarter:	1981	1980	1979	1978
Mar.	1,348	1,225	1,104	888
Jun.	1,443	1,197	1,347	1,134
Sep.	1,410	1,278	1,385	1,203
Dec.	1,222	1,316	1,371	1,178
	5,414	5,016	5,207	4,403

Based on the preliminary report, sales for 1981 rose 7.9% from those of 1980. However, profitability was hurt by the prolonged housing slump, and pretax income fell 34%. After taxes at 30.4%, against 30.8%, net income was also off 34%. Share profits equaled $1.51, versus $2.33.

Common Share Earnings ($)

Quarter:	1981	1980	1979	1978
Mar.	0.49	0.48	0.71	0.62
Jun.	0.52	0.53	0.92	0.82
Sep.	0.29	0.71	0.82	0.76
Dec.	0.21	0.62	0.67	0.73
	1.51	2.34	3.12	2.93

Important Developments

Jan. '82—GP said that it would ask the U.S. Supreme Court to review an unfavorable decision by a lower court in a plywood antitrust suit. In September, 1981 an appeals court in New Orleans upheld a 1978 jury verdict which found GP, Weyerhaeuser and Willamette Industries guilty of fixing plywood prices. GP added that while it was unlikely that the ultimate outcome of this matter would have a material adverse effect on its financial position, such a consequence was possible. The company's auditors plan to qualify their opinion on GP's 1981 financial statements subject to the outcome of this litigation.

Dec. '81—GP arranged $650 million of revolving credit facilities with domestic and foreign banks.

Next earnings report due in mid-April.

Per Share Data ($)

Yr. End Dec. 31	1981	1980	1979	1978	1977	1976	1975	1974	1973	1972
Book Value	**NA**	19.02	17.85	16.79	14.88	13.17	10.71	9.64	8.35	7.06
Earnings[1]	**[2]1.51**	[2]2.34	[2]3.12	[2]2.93	[2]2.54	[2]2.12	[2]1.54	[2]1.76	[2]1.82	1.05
Dividends	**1.20**	1.20	1.12½	1.02½	0.83½	0.70¼	0.49⅜	0.47½	0.46	0.44⅞
Payout Ratio	**79%**	51%	35%	35%	33%	33%	32%	27%	25%	43%
Prices—High	**32⅜**	34⅞	30⅜	32½	37	37⅜	29⅝	26⅞	26½	28½
Low	**17¾**	21½	23½	23½	25¼	26⅜	15½	13⅜	17¼	20¼
P/E Ratio—	**21-12**	15-9	10-8	11-8	15-10	18-12	19-10	15-8	15-9	27-19

Data as orig. reptd. Adj. for stk. div(s). of 2% Aug. 1977, 2% Feb. 1977, 50% Aug. 1976, 2% Jan. 1976, 2% Aug. 1975, 2% Feb. 1975, 2% Aug. 1974, 2% Jan. 1974, 1% Jul. 1973, 1% Feb. 1973, 1% Aug. 1972, 1% Feb. 1972. **1.** Bef. spec. item(s) of –0.06 in 1973. **2.** Ful. dil.: 1.49 in 1981, 2.28 in 1980, 3.03 in 1979, 2.84 in 1978, 2.47 in 1977, 2.05 in 1976, 1.48 in 1975, 1.69 in 1974, 1.74 in 1973. NA-Not Available.

Standard NYSE Stock Reports
Vol. 49/No. 27/Sec. 10

February 9, 1982

Standard & Poor's Corp.
25 Broadway, NY, NY 10004

1006

Georgia-Pacific Corporation

Income Data (Million $)

Year Ended Dec. 31	Revs.	Oper. Inc.	% Oper. Inc. of Revs.	Cap. Exp.	Depr.	Int. Exp.	Net Bef. Taxes	Eff. Tax Rate	[4]Net Inc.	% Net Inc. of Revs.
1980	**5,016**	**720**	**14.4%**	**[5]584**	**288**	**138**	**353**	**30.9%**	**244**	**4.9%**
1979	5,207	847	16.3%	878	245	103	536	39.0%	327	6.3%
1978	4,403	776	17.6%	527	208	64	530	43.0%	302	6.9%
1977	3,675	673	18.3%	490	187	51	453	42.2%	262	7.1%
1976	3,038	556	18.3%	318	162	51	356	39.6%	215	7.1%
1975	2,359	423	18.0%	277	[2]142	69	232	36.1%	148	6.3%
1974	2,432	456	18.8%	331	131	80	264	37.8%	164	6.8%
1973	2,229	469	21.0%	359	129	61	287	41.2%	169	7.6%
[1]1972	1,774	318	17.9%	201	106	42	170	42.4%	98	5.5%
1971	1,447	281	19.4%	216	108	44	[3]130	33.8%	86	6.0%

Balance Sheet Data (Million $)

Dec. 31	Cash	——Current—— Assets	Liab.	Ratio	Total Assets	Ret. on Assets	Long Term Debt	Common Equity	Total Cap.	% LT Debt of Cap.	Ret. on Equity
1980	**32.0**	**1,195**	**770**	**1.6**	**4,512**	**5.6%**	**1,227**	**1,879**	**3,740**	**32.8%**	**12.7%**
1979	22.0	1,123	661	1.7	4,118	8.9%	1,109	1,760	3,448	32.2%	18.6%
1978	21.0	944	461	2.0	3,344	9.6%	827	1,726	2,878	28.7%	18.6%
1977	11.0	825	378	2.2	2,929	9.5%	732	1,529	2,541	28.8%	18.2%
1976	25.6	753	533	1.4	2,584	8.4%	443	1,352	2,045	21.7%	17.6%
1975	48.3	682	254	2.7	2,404	6.3%	907	1,028	2,150	42.2%	15.2%
1974	68.8	628	291	2.2	2,231	7.8%	873	897	1,935	45.1%	19.6%
1973	58.8	589	258	2.3	2,002	9.1%	831	774	1,741	47.8%	23.6%
1972	56.5	506	213	2.4	1,700	5.4%	717	653	1,487	48.2%	14.3%
1971	87.4	540	211	2.6	1,873	4.7%	836	696	1,655	50.5%	12.9%

Data as orig. reptd. **1.** Excludes discontinued operations. **2.** Reflects accounting change. **3.** Incl. equity in earns. of nonconsol. subs. **4.** Bef. spec. item(s) in 1973. **5.** Net of curr. yr. retirement and disposals.

Business Summary

Georgia Pacific is the largest domestic producer of plywood, with major interests in the lumber, paper, chemical and gypsum fields. GP operates over 230 plants in the U.S., Canada, the Philippines, Indonesia and Brazil. Industry segment contributions in 1980:

	Sales	Profits
Building products	58%	34%
Pulp, paper & paperboard	28%	30%
Chemicals	13%	33%
Other	1%	3%

Building products include softwood plywood and specialties (particleboard, insulation board, hardboard and panelboard), lumber, and gypsum products, which are sold through some 165 distribution centers in the U.S. and Canada.

GP operates 26 primary pulp and paper plants with an aggregate capacity of about 3,000,000 tons, as well as 38 converting plants. Products include bags and sacks, tissues, paperboard and corrugated containers.

Over 50 chemical plants are operated, which produce resin, formaldehyde, lignin and various other products. Exchange Oil and Gas explores for and develops oil and gas properties in the Gulf of Mexico.

GP owns about 4.5 million acres of timberland in North America, with cutting rights on another 600,000 acres. GP also owns 800,000 acres in Brazil and has joint ownership on cutting rights on 1,700,000 acres in Indonesia. GP obtains some 50% of its net fiber needs from its own holdings.

Dividend Data

Dividends have been paid since 1927. A dividend reinvestment plan is available.

Amt. of Divd. $	Date Decl.	Ex-divd. Date	Stock of Record	Payment Date
0.30	May 5	May 11	May 15	Jun. 15'81
0.30	Jul. 27	Aug. 3	Aug. 7	Sep. 8'81
0.30	Oct. 28	Oct. 30	Nov. 6	Dec. 7'81
0.30	Jan. 25	Feb. 1	Feb. 5	Mar. 8'82

Capitalization

Long Term Debt: $1,368,000,000.

$2.24 Conv. Pfd. Stk.: 6,097,000 shs. in 3 series; conv. sh.-for-sh. into com.

Common Stock: 105,520,000 shs. ($0.80 par). Institutions hold some 41%. Shareholders: 91,600.

Office—900 Southwest Fifth Ave., Portland, Ore. 97204. **Tel**—(503) 222-5561. **Chrmn & CEO**—R. E. Flowerree. **Pres**—T. M. Hahn, Jr. **Secy**—M. A. McCravey. **Treas**—M. L. Talmadge. **Investor Contact**—R. A. Good. **Dirs**—W. S. Boothby, Jr., A. J. Bows, J. N. Cheatham, R. L. Clare, Jr., R. E. Flowerree, H. C. Freuhauf, Jr., T. M. Hahn, Jr., F. Jungers, H. J. Kane, R. E. McNair, C. J. Medberry, H. E. Sand, R. A. Schumacher, J. F. Watlington, Jr. **Transfer Agent & Registrar**—Bank of America, San Francisco. **Incorporated** in Ga. in 1927.

As you can see on page 132, each report includes a summary of the company's business, its current outlook, earnings and so on. It is likely that you will be asked to send copies of these reports to clients. (The procedure for doing so will be covered in an exercise at the end of this lesson.)

Standard & Poor's Dividend Record Book

The *Standard & Poor's Dividend Record Book* lists dividends and stock splits, and is used to research dividend problems. The publication provides the record date, ex-dividend date and payable date for all dividends and stock splits on publicly traded securities. The book is organized into three sections:

1. a *Daily Dividend*—a daily updated record of dividends;

2. a *Weekly Cumulative Dividend*—a weekly update; and

3. a *Main Cumulative Dividend*—a year-to-date recording.

The filing procedure for this publication is noteworthy. The *Daily Dividend Section* is filed until the *Weekly Cumulative Section* is compiled. The dailies are then thrown out and the weekly section is retained until it is replaced by the *Main Cumulative Section* and so on. Eventually, an annual book covering the entire year is compiled.

Standard & Poor's Corporation Record Book

Yet another decision-making tool is the *Standard & Poor's Corporation Records Book*. It is comprised of two sections. The first section is called *Current News Edition* and serves as an index to the most recently added news items. The second section of the *Corporation Record Book* provides information arranged alphabetically by company name.

National Stock Summary

Another outside publication likely to be used in the branch office is the *National Stock Summary*. This publication contains company information such as:

- the par value of the stock;
- the name of the transfer agent;
- the terms of any mergers; and
- the address of the company.

The *National Stock Summary* is often used to gather information relative to defunct companies, merged companies, and over-the-counter securities.

Internal Publications

As previously mentioned, there are two kinds of publications that you will be using: outside and internal. No doubt your firm has a number of publications which are useful in helping your account executive, as well as his/her clients make investment decisions. They may include brochures describing your firm's products (such as IRAs, Keogh plans, annuities, mutual bond funds, and so on) or they may be your company newsletter, new product bulletins or the like.

As sales assistant you need to know how each publication is to be used, as well as how and where to get them. The exercises on the new few pages should help you carry out any publication-related responsibilities you may have in your branch.

NOTE: You may want to use the form at the end of this lesson to record responses in the following exercises. Make one photocopy of the form for each publication listed above, fill in your account executive's responses to the questions, and clip a sample of the publication to the form for future reference.

EXERCISE 11:1
Publications

████████████████████████████████████

Using the
Standard & Poor's Reports (S&P Sheets)

Locate your branch's *Standard & Poor's Reports* volumes. (There should be three sets of books in the branch; one set for each exchange: NYSE, AMEX and OTC.) Read the instructions on how to use the reports (see the first few pages of the first volume in any one of the three sets). Then enter the appropriate information in the space below.

1. Find the report on *Philip Morris Companies* and enter the page number of the report here: _____

2. Find the report on *Niagara Mohawk Power Company* and enter the page number of the report here: _____

3. Find the report on *Integrated Software Systems Company (ISSCO)* and enter the page number of the report here:

_____

4. List the steps you followed in accessing the reports.

a. _____

b. _____

c. _____

d. _____

e. _____

f. _____

Ask your account executive for feedback on the above. Make corrections, if necessary, on this page.

Your branch may have a specific policy regarding the use of this publication. Ask your account executive the following questions and enter the appropriate information in the space provided.

Should I send original reports or copies to clients?

_____

If originals are sent, who does the reordering needed to get replacement reports?

_____

NOTE: If you send out originals, be sure that you notify the person responsible for reordering reports.

**EXERCISE 11:2
Publications**

Using the
Standard & Poor's Dividend Record Book

Locate your branch's *Standard & Poor's Dividend Record Book*. (Note that the book is organized into three sections: *Daily Dividend, Weekly Cumulative Dividend* and *Main Cumulative Dividend*.) Read the instructions on how to use the book (located at front of book). Then ask your account executive the following questions and enter the appropriate information in the space provided.

1. When would I need to consult this book?

_____

_____

_____

2. The book is used to research dividend problems; what kinds of problems would I be using the book for?

_____

_____

_____

_____

_____

3. Would you give me a typical question or problem to address which requires the use of this book? (Write the question/problem below.)

_____

_____

(Address the question/problem based on your prior reading of the instructions. Ask your account executive for help, if necessary. Take notes in the space below for future reference.)

_____

_____

_____

_____

_____

4. Are there any other typical questions or problems which I should practice answering in this exercise? (If so, you should try to work them out yourself, using the space below, while the account executive looks on. Be sure to ask for help if *anything* is unclear to you.)

EXERCISE 11:3
Publications

Using the
Standard & Poor's Corporation Records Book

Locate your branch's *Standard & Poor's Corporation Records Book*. (Note that the book is divided into two sections: *Current News Edition* and information on companies alphabetized by company name.) Read the instructions on how to use the book (located at front of book). Then ask your account executive the following questions and enter the appropriate information in the space provided.

1. When would I need to consult this book?

_____

_____

_____

2. The book is used as a research and information tool; what kinds of questions would I be using the book to answer?

_____

_____

_____

_____

_____

3. Would you give me a typical question to address which requires the use of this book? (Write the question below.)

_____

_____

(Address the question based on your prior reading of the instructions. Ask your account executive for help, if necessary. Take notes in the space below for future reference.)

_____

_____

_____

_____

_____

_____

4. Are there any other typical questions which I should practice
     answering in this exercise? (If so, you should try to work them
     out yourself, using the space below, while the account execu-
     tive looks on. Be sure to ask for help if *anything* is unclear to
     you.)

     _____

     _____

     _____

     _____

     _____

     _____

     _____

     _____

     _____

     _____

     _____

     _____

EXERCISE 11:4
Publications

Using the
National Stock Summary

Locate your branch's *National Stock Summary.* Read the instructions on how to use the book (located at the front of the book). Then ask your account executive the following questions and enter the appropriate information in the space provided.

1. When would I need to consult this book?

_____

_____

_____

2. The *National Stock Summary* can be used to look up defunct companies, merged companies and over-the-counter securities; what kinds of questions would I be using the book to answer?

_____

_____

_____

_____

_____

3. Would you give me a typical question to address which requires the use of this book? (Write the question below.)

_____

_____

(Address the question based on your prior reading of the instructions. Ask your account executive for help, if necessary. Take notes in the space below for future reference.)

_____

_____

_____

_____

_____

_____

4. Are there any other typical questions which I should practice answering in this exercise? (If so, you should try to answer them yourself, using the space below, while your account executive looks on. Be sure to ask for help if anything is *unclear* to you.)

_____

_____

_____

_____

_____

_____

_____

_____

_____

_____

_____

_____

EXERCISE 11:5
Publications

━━━━━━━━━━━━━━━━━━━━━━━━━━━━━━━━━

Internal Publications

See your account executive for answers to the following internal publication questions. Enter the appropriate information in the space provided.

What internal publications used in our branch do I need to know?

(Collect all publications and *enter their names and publication numbers in the space below* before proceeding. You will need this information when requesting additional copies of brochures, newsletters, etc.)

_____ _____

_____ _____

_____ _____

_____ _____

_____ _____

_____ _____

_____ _____

_____ _____

_____ _____

_____ _____

For each publication ask your account executive:

- What is its purpose?
- How is it used?
- Who should get it?
- Should I give out originals or copies?
- Whom do I contact for more originals?

FORM 11:1
Publications

Internal Publications

Publication Name _____

Publication Number _____

Its purpose: _____

_____

_____

How it is used: _____

_____

_____

Who should get it: _____

_____

_____

_____

_____

_____

Give out: Originals _____   or   Copies _____

_____

_____

Contact _____ for more originals.
       name   ph. no.

NOTES:

Steps to Buy/Sell a Security

In this lesson we will focus on the mechanics of your branch's most important activity—the buying and selling of securities. We will cover your related duties for buy or sell trades.

These duties include:

- verifying the accuracy of trades; and
- helping to correct any errors.

Let's now examine what happens when a client calls your account executive with an order to buy or sell a security.

Steps to Buying and Selling a Security

First the account executive completes an order ticket like the one in Figure 12-1. Every order contains information as to the type of order (buy/sell), the quantity and a description of the security, and all the necessary account data. If there are other requirements, they will appear on the order, as well. (More on this later in this lesson.)

B U Y

STOCK EXCHANGES						BONDS			BLOCK DEPT	FINAN SERV DEPT	SYNDI-CATE	MUTUAL FUNDS	SPECIAL HAND'NG	OTHER	ORDER NUMBER	OFFICE	EXECUTED PRICE
NYSE & ASE	NASDAQ	OVER THE CNTR	CHI'GO MID-WEST	PACIFIC COAST	BOSTON P-B-W	CORP-ORATE	MUNI-CIPAL	CONV-ERTIBLE									$25\frac{1}{8}$
NAX	OTC ☑	OTN	CMW	PCX	HEND	BND	BMUN	CONV	ID	FND	STIC	CGE	SHD				

0

☐ POSS DUPE   ☑ **BUY**   ATTN:

1

QUANTITY	SYMBOL OR DESCRIPTION	SUFFIX*	PRICE OR MARKET	STOP	STOP LIMIT PRICE	TYPE OF ORDER OTHER THAN LIMITED OR MARKET
100	*MED*		MKT	☐ STP	____ LMT	☐ BAS ☐ OB ☐ WITH DISCRETION ☐ WOW ☐ CLO

2

3   ☐ AON ☐ N H ☐ DAY ☑ GTC ☐ OPG ☐ FOK ☐ OC   ☐ DNR ☐ CASH ☐ ND   **PRINCIPAL TRANSACTION**

4   ☐ POSS DUPE   ☐ OR ☐ SW ☐ CXL ☐ BUY   ☐ INFORM CUSTOMER WE MAKE MARKET

QUANTITY	SYMBOL OR DESCRIPTION	SUFFIX*	PRICE OR MARKET	STOP	STOP LIMIT PRICE	
				☐ STP	____ LMT	☐ BAS ☐ OB ☐ WITH DISCRETION ☐ WOW ☐ CLO

5

6   LVS   ☐ AON ☐ NH ☐ DAY ☐ GTC ☐ OPG ☐ FOK ☐ OC ☐ DNR ☐ CASH ☐ ND   ☑ CHECK IF NEW ACCOUNT

OFFICE	ACCOUNT NUMBER	TYPE	TYPE OF ACCOUNT	SPLIT SHARES	DISCRETIONARY NYSE RULE 408	EMPLOYEE	A.E. NO.	MGR'S APPROVAL
J S L	9 8 7 6 5	2	P-CASH 1-CASH 2-MARGIN 3-SHORT 4-SPEC. SUBSCRIPTION 5-CONV BOND 6-SPEC. BOND			*JSD*	*42*	*AM*

7

8   CXL'S ONLY   REF   ORIG STATION   MESSAGE NO.   CUSTOMER NAME *JAMES KEARNEY*

9   COM   ☐ A.E. OVERRIDE [R/ _ _ _]   ☐ NEG. ¢ PER SH [M/90 _ _ _]   ☐ NEG. DISC. [CD _ _ %]   ☐ ST INS OVERRIDE [I/ _]

10   COM   ☐ SPECIAL DESCRIPTIVE INST. [D/ _____]   ☐ D/UNSOL

11   COM

12   COM

13   CONFIRM LINE CFN LINE 2 & 5

SUFFIX CODES
CALLED CL
CERTIFICATE CT
CLASS OF AB
SECURITY ETC
CONVERTIBLE CV
FOREIGN F
PREFERRED PR
RIGHTS RT
SPECIAL SP
STAMPED SD
WHEN
DISTRIBUTED WD
WHEN
ISSUED WI
WITH
WARRANTS WW
WITHOUT
WARRANTS XW
WARRANTS WS

ORDER COPY

Figure 12-1. An Order Ticket.

Upon receipt of the order, the order room's *CRT operator* routes the order to the exchange or *point of execution*. A *broker* on the floor of the exchange or a *trader* in the OTC market executes the order and sends an *execution report*, which specifies time of the execution plus the order information, to the CRT operator who matches or compares the execution report to the order ticket. The CRT operator then sends a copy of the report to the account executive who checks the report for any errors.

Upon receipt of the order, the order room *CRT operator* routes the order to the exchange or *point of execution*. A *trader* on the floor of the exchange executes the order and sends an *execution report,* which specifies time of the execution plus the order information, to the CRT operator who matches or compares the execution report to the order ticket. The CRT operator then sends a copy of the report to the account executive who checks the report for any errors.

Next the account executive reports (by telephone) the execution price to the client. The following morning the client's confirmation is received in the branch via computer printout and *the sales assistant double checks its accuracy.*

Once the trade is executed, the *purchase and sales* department begins the processing cycle. This department records the completed transactions, figures the amount due from the buyer and/or to the seller, and prepares the confirmation. The branch P&S clerk checks the confirmation against the execution report for errors. See Figure 12-2.

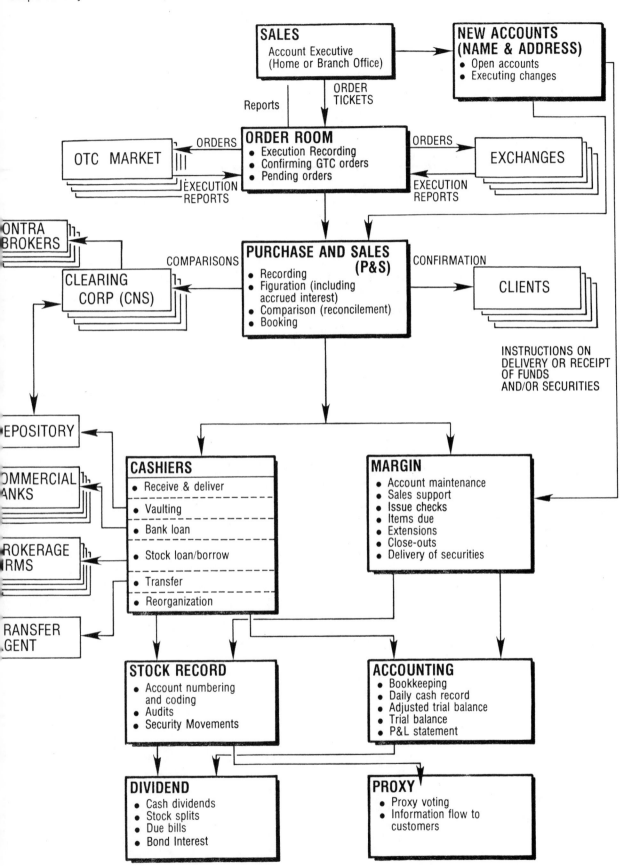

Figure 12-2. A Typical Operations Organization Chart.

More on Orders

Orders were merely referred to in the above information. You will need knowledge of the following information concerning orders to carry out your duties.

Every order that comes from an account executive must contain certain information:

- type of order—buy, sell long, or sell short;
- quantity of trade;
- description of the security to be transacted; and
- customer's account number and name.

This information allows the employees in the order room and at the place of execution to know which security is to be traded, what quantity is involved, and whether the client is buying or selling the security. The customer's name or account number is necessary for the later processing of the order, as well as for satisfying certain rules and regulations.

Through buying or selling securities, customers are attempting to attain goals. That is, they are looking to buy or sell at a certain price in order to lock in a profit and so on. To aid them, different types of order instructions are at their disposal. Each type of order uses additional information that custom-tailors it to the needs and wishes of the customer.

A *market order* is an order to execute at whatever the market price is when the account executive enters the exchange. A *buy market order* accepts the current offer. A *sell market order* accepts the bid as it stands.

A *limit order* puts a limit on the price that the customer is willing to pay or receive. A *buy limit order* establishes the highest price that the customer is willing to pay. This means that the order can be executed at the limit price or lower. A *sell limit order* sets the lowest price that the customer is willing to accept. This order can be executed at the limit price or higher.

A *stop order* is a written order that becomes a market order when the price on the order ticket is reached or passed. A *buy stop order* is entered *above* the current market, and a *sell limit order* is entered *below* it. All stop orders could be executed immediately if it weren't for the stop instruction on the memorandum.

Example: John Doe buys 100 shares of RAM at $55 per share. He does not have access to a *tape* or *quote machine* and cannot watch the price movement of the security, but wants to risk no more than $500 on this transaction. John could enter an order to "Sell 100 RAM at 50 *stop.*" Because the market is now 55, John's order would be executed immediately if it were not for the stop instruction on the order. With the word "stop," the market has to fall to 50 or below before this order can be executed.

There are other orders which are entered for special purposes. Let's take just a quick look at each:

1. *Stop Limit*—the same as stop order, but it becomes a limit order instead of a market order when the stop price is reached.

2. *Fill-or-Kill (FOK)*—must be executed in its entirety immediately or it's cancelled.

3. *Immediate or Cancel (IOC)*—any part of the order may be executed immediately and the rest cancelled.

4. *All-or-None (AON)*—time constraints, such as a day, demand that *all* of the shares must be filled or the client does not have to accept the execution.

Option Orders

5. *Spread Order*—contains the instruction to buy one product or issue and simultaneously sell the same with different terms. For example, "B (buy) 1 call ZAP Apr 40, S (sell) 1 call ZAP Apr 45." These are usually used in listed options and futures trading.

6. *Straddle Order*—the simultaneous purchase or sale of a put and a call on the same underlying stock in the same series. These are usually used in listed options. For example, "B (buy) 1 call WIP Jul 60, B (buy) 1 put WIP Jul 60." Straddle orders also apply to certain future transactions.

7. *Combination Order*—similar to a straddle, but it uses a different series designation.

8. *One Cancels Other (OCO)*—has two possible executions. The first one to get executed automatically cancels the other. Hence its name: one cancels other.

9. *GTC orders (good-till-cancelled)*—stay "open" until they are executed or the customer cancels them.

Your Duties

Relative to the buy/sell process, the sales assistant's duties include helping his/her account executive in answering clients' questions and verifying the accuracy of trades. Your account executive will help familiarize you with the specifics as you complete the exercises at the end of this lesson. But first, check your understanding of the buy/sell process by taking the following quiz.

QUIZ 12:1
Steps to Buy/Sell a Security

The steps to buying and selling a security are presented below in Column 2. However, the steps are out of order. Put the steps in the proper order by entering the letter of each step in the appropriate blank in Column 1.

Column 1   Column 2

1. ___

2. ___

3. ___

4. ___

5. ___

6. ___

7. ___

8. ___

9. ___

10. ___

a. The account executive takes an order to buy or sell from the client.

b. A broker on the exchange floor executes the order.

c. The order room CRT operator routes the order to the exchange.

d. The account executive reports (by telephone) the execution price to the client.

e. The account executive sends the completed order ticket to the order room.

f. The client's confirmation is received in the branch (via printout) and the sales assistant double checks its accuracy.

g. The branch P&S clerk checks the confirmation against the execution report for errors.

h. An execution report is transmitted from the exchange to the order room CRT operator who matches or compares the execution report to the order ticket.

i. The account executive receives and checks the execution report for any errors.

j. The confirmation is mailed to the client.

11. List the basic information that must be included in an account executive's order:

a. _____

b. _____

c. _____

d. _____

12. Define each of these terms:

a. market order   _____

b. buy market order   _____

c. sell market order   _____

d. limit order   _____

e. buy limit order   _____

f. sell limit order   _____

g. stop order   _____

h. buy stop order   _____

i. sell stop order   _____

j. stop limit   _____

k. fill or kill   _____
l. immediate order
   cancel   _____

m. all or none   _____

n. spread order   _____

o. straddle order   _____
p. combination
   order   _____

q. one cancels
   other   _____
r. good-till-
   cancelled (GTC)   _____

NOTES:

_____

_____

_____

_____

_____

_____

_____

_____

_____

_____

_____

_____

_____

_____

_____

_____

_____

_____

_____

_____

_____

_____

_____

_____

_____

_____

_____

_____

_____

_____

_____

QUIZ ANSWERS 12:1

Steps to Buy/Sell a Security

1. <u>a</u>
2. <u>e</u>
3. <u>c</u>
4. <u>b</u>
5. <u>h</u>
6. <u>i</u>
7. <u>d</u>
8. <u>f</u>
9. <u>g</u>
10. <u>j</u>
11. List the basic information that must be included in an account executive's order:

    a. Whether the order is to buy, sell long, or sell short.

    b. The quantity.

    c. A description of the security to be transacted.

    d. The customer's account number and usually the account name.

12. Define each of these terms:

a. market order	an order to execute at whatever the market price is when the account executive enters the crowd.
b. buy market order	accepts the current order.
c. sell market order	accepts the bid.
d. limit order	puts a limit on the price that the client will accept.
e. buy limit order	sets the highest price someone is willing to pay.
f. sell limit order	sets the lowest price someone is willing to pay.
g. stop order	a memorandum that becomes a market order when the price on the order ticket is reached or passed.
h. buy stop order	is entered above the current market.
i. sell stop order	is entered below it.
j. stop limit	the same as stop order, but it becomes a limit order instead of a market order when the stop price is reached.
k. fill or kill	this order must be executed in its entirety immediately or it's cancelled.
l. immediate or cancel	any part of the order may be executed immediately and the rest cancelled.
m. all or none	given time constraints, such as a day, all of the order must be filled or the client does not have to accept the execution.
n. spread order	used in options and futures trading, this order includes the instruction to buy one product or issue and simultaneously sell the same with different terms.
o. straddle order	used in listed options, this is the simultaneous purchase or sale of a put and a call on the same underlying stock in the same series.
p. combination order	similar to a straddle, but it uses a different series designation.
q. one cancels other	has two possible executions; the first one to get executed automatically cancels the other.
r. good-till-cancelled (GTC)	orders which stay open until they are executed or the client cancels them.

EXERCISE 12:1
Steps to Buy/Sell a Security

The steps to buy or sell a security are listed below. Ask your account executive to point out any differences between the steps which apply to your branch and those shown here. Be sure to note the differences on this sheet.

Afterwards, proceed through *each* step, asking yourself *who, what, where, when, why,* and *how*. For some steps, the answers will be obvious to you, but it's likely that you will need assistance from your account executive to fully understand the workings of some steps in your branch. Be sure to ask for clarification.

1. The account executive takes an order to buy or sell from the client.

_____

_____

_____

2. The account executive sends the completed order ticket to the order room.

_____

_____

_____

3. The order room CRT operator routes the order to the exchange.

_____

_____

_____

4. A trader on the exchange floor executes the order.

_____

_____

_____

5. An execution report is transmitted from the exchange to the order room CRT operator who matches or compares the execution report to the order ticket.

_____

_____

_____

6. The account executive receives and checks the execution report for any errors.

_____

_____

_____

7. The account executive reports (by telephone) the execution price to the client.

_____

_____

_____

8. The client's confirmation is received in the branch (via printout) and the sales assistant double checks its accuracy.

_____

_____

_____

9. The branch P&S clerk checks the confirmation against the execution report for errors.

_____

_____

_____

10. The confirmation is mailed to the client.

_____

_____

_____

EXERCISE 12:2

Steps to Buy/Sell a Security

As mentioned earlier in this lesson, your duties relative to buying and selling securities are to verify the accuracy of trades and help to correct any errors, as well as answer client questions. To help you do so, ask your account executive for copies of an order ticket and its execution report. Review each item, asking your account executive for clarification wherever needed.

Afterwards, take another look at the steps to buying and selling securities as outlined in Exercise 12:1. For each step, ask your account executive to specify your duties and note them below. (Confirmations will be discussed in the next lesson.)

The Sales Assistant's Duties

1. _____
   _____

2. _____
   _____

3. _____
   _____

4. _____
   _____

5. _____
   _____

6. _____
   _____

7. _____
   _____

8. _____
   _____

9. _____
   _____

10. _____
    _____

SECTION 13
Confirmation

When an account executive completes a trade for a client, he/she personally notifies the client, usually by telephone. But the client also receives written notice of the execution from the brokerage firm. This written notice is known as the customer's *confirmation*.

The confirmation, whether computer generated or manually typed, carries a detailed description of the trade as you will see in this section. This description must be accurate to ensure proper service to the client, and *it is your responsibility to check out and correct any errors.*

Customer confirmations are usually prepared the night the trade is processed and mailed the next morning. Additional copies of the confirmation are sent to the account executive and certain operating departments for information and record retention purposes.

When the branch office receives a copy of the customer confirmation, the sales assistant should verify all aspects of the confirmation. This includes checking:

- details of the trade;
- the client's name and address; and
- any special instructions.

To ensure accuracy, the sales assistant should verify every confirmation against the original ticket and make sure that all instructions have been followed.

Elements of a Confirmation

In reviewing the following elements of a written confirmation, use the glossary to look up any unfamiliar terms:

1. trade date (actual day the trade occurred);

2. settlement date (day the terms of the trade are to be completed);

3. transaction type (buy or sell);

4. quantity;

5. security description;

6. price;

7. first money (comparison money including accrued interest when applicable);

8. commission (agency);

9. SEC fee (listed sales);

10. net money;

11. where trade was executed;

12. capacity in which firm is acting (agency, principal, firm as market maker);

13. account's name and address; and

14. any special instructions such as:

a) transfer and ship;

b) delivery versus payment:

- Delivery instructions;

- Delivery address;

c) transfer and hold.

Naturally you must be familiar with the confirmations used in your branch in order to effectively carry out your responsibility of checking out and correcting any errors. An exercise which will cover all aspects of your branch's confirmation is provided at the end of this lesson, but first please complete the following brief quiz.

Stone, Forrest & Rivers	OFFICE ACCOUNT NO.	TYPE	A E	TRADE DATE	SETTLEMENT DATE	TRANS. NO.	CUSIP NO.	EXCH	ORIG	S

YOU BOUGHT	YOU SOLD	SECURITY DESCRIPTION					

GROSS AMOUNT

PRICE

INTEREST
COMMISSION
STATE TAX
SERVICE CHG.
SEC/POST
AMOUNT DUE ✱
SYMBOL

PLEASE RETURN SECOND COPY

WITH SECURITIES SOLD (IF IN YOUR POSSESSION) OR WITH AMOUNT DUE ✱ (IF NOT ALREADY IN YOUR ACCOUNT)

BY SETTLEMENT DATE
IN THE ENCLOSED ENVELOPE

IN ACCORDANCE WITH YOUR INSTRUCTIONS WE ARE PLEASED TO CONFIRM THE ABOVE TRANSACTION FOR YOUR ACCOUNT AND RISK SUBJECT TO TERMS LISTED ON REVERSE SIDE.

Figure 13-1. A typical confirmation.

QUIZ 13:1
Confirmation

For each item, write the appropriate response in the space provided.

1. What is a confirmation?

_____

2. What is your responsibility relative to confirmations?

_____

3. When are confirmations usually prepared?

_____

4. When are confirmations usually mailed?

_____

5. Confirmations should be verified by checking them against the

_____.

6. How much of the information included on the confirmation must be checked by the sales assistant? _____

QUIZ ANSWERS 13:1

Confirmation

1. What is a confirmation?
A written notice to the client confirming the execution of a trade.
2. What is your responsibility relative to confirmations?
To check out and correct any errors.
3. When are confirmations usually prepared?
The night the trade is processed.
4. When are confirmations usually mailed?
The next morning.
5. Confirmations should be verified by checking them against the original ticket.
6. How much of the information included on the confirmation must be checked by the sales assistant? All of it.

See your branch operations manager of your account executive to get a *photocopy* of a confirmation issued to one of your branch customers. Study the front and back of the confirmation. For each element listed below, write its corresponding number next to the element on the photocopied confirmation. When you finish ask the operations manager or the account executive to review with you each element of your branch's confirmation (both front and back).

You need to know every element of the confirmation so you will be able to answer client questions promptly and accurately. They are as follows:

1. trade date;

2. settlement date;

3. transaction type (buy or sell);

4. quantity;

5. security description;

6. price;

7. first money (comparison money including accrued interest when applicable);

8. commission (agency);

9. SEC fee (listed sales);

10. net money;

11. where trade was executed;

12. capacity in which firm is acting (agency, principal, firm as market maker);

13. account's name and address;

14. any special instructions:

    a) transfer and ship;

    b) delivery versus payment:

        1. Delivery instructions;

        2. Delivery address;

    c) transfer and hold.

NOTES:

Securities Explained

In this lesson, we will cover various types of securities and how you will work with them in your branch. The main securities that we will cover are:

1. Three forms of business ownership:
- proprietorship;
- partnership; and
- corporation.

2. Three forms of business securities:
- common stock;
- preferred stock; and
- bonds.

3. Four types of corporate bonds:
- mortgage;
- collateral trust;
- equipment trust; and
- debenture.

4. Bond features:
- serial bond;
- income (adjustment) bond;
- sinking fund bonds; and
- convertible bonds.

5. Bond certificates.

6. Municipal bonds:
- general obligation bonds; and
- revenue bonds.

7. Government securities:
- Treasury bills;
- notes; and
- bonds.

8. Federal agency securities:
- Fannie Mae;
- Ginnie Mae;
- Sallie Mae and others.

What are Securities?

Knowing the language of the securities industry is the sales assistant's passport to any brokerage office. Accurate communication depends on this essential skill. Clients, account executives and everybody else in the office expects you to have a common understanding of financial terms. And it's the sales assistant's responsibility to learn all of the terminology in use today.

This chapter defines just some basic terms. If you want more information, many other books available today explain a wider range of terms and the economic principles behind them. Current periodicals keep the industry up with new usages and most of the new terms and concepts. Business, tax and government news give additional shades of meaning to the old terms. Knowing the language is an ongoing process that requires each sales assistant to read, talk and live the industry in which he/she works and want to succeed.

Key Definitions

There are three primary forms of business ownership:

1. the proprietorship;

2. the partnership; and

3. the corporation.

The Proprietorship
This is a business that is owned and operated by one person.

The Partnership
This is a business that is owned and operated by two or more persons.

The Corporation

This is a business where ownership is represented by some form of security. Many people own the business (through corporate stock) and, collectively, they select a management team to operate it.

There are three basic forms of corporate securities:

1. common stock;

2. preferred stock; and

3. bonds.

Common Stock

Stock is a security that represents ownership, or equity, in a corporation. Stock is sold in units called *shares*. Common stock entitles the owner to voting rights on management, certain other issues, and dividends in proportion to the number of shares owned.

Formation of Stock. One aspect of developing a corporation charter is to define the characteristics of the stock including: number of shares to be issued, type of stock, and par value.

Dividends. Owners of common stock are given dividends only after the owners of bonds and preferred stocks receive theirs.

Liquidation of the Corporation. Owners of common stock get their share of corporate assets after the interests of preferred stockholders and bondholders are satisfied. The liabilities of a common stockholder are limited to the purchase price of the stock.

Preferred Stock

This type of stock also shows ownership and an equity position with the corporation. However, owners of preferred stock do not have any vote on management or on key issues, but they do receive dividends before the common stockholders receive theirs.

Dividends. Preferred stocks are supposed to pay a fixed rate of dividend. The rate is expressed either as a *dollar amount* or as a *percentage*. The dollar amount is the amount to be paid per share per year. The percentage is a percentage of the par value of a security, not the selling price.

Liquidation. Preferred stockholders have a prior claim over common stockholders to the assets of a corporation should it be dissolved.

Types of Preferred Stock. Once a decision is made to issue a preferred stock, corporate officials offer certain features to make the preferred attractive to the public.

- *Dividend rates.* The dividend must be competitive with other similar companies and other fixed income securities.
- *Cumulative/noncumulative.* If the preferred is *noncumulative,* a dividend that is not paid is lost forever. If the preferred is *cumulative,* all dividends that have been missed and the current dividend must be paid before the common stockholder can receive a dividend.
- *Callable.* When the preferred is *callable,* the corporation can "call in" the stock and retire it for a predetermined price.
- *Convertible.* When the preferred is *convertible* it can be converted at the stockholder's option into common stock at a specific conversion rate.

Treasury Stock. Shares that are reacquired through purchase, and occasionally by donation, are identified as *treasury stock.* No dividends or voting rights are assigned to these stocks once they are reacquired.

Common Stock, Par Value. For bookkeeping purposes, each share of stock is assigned a *par value.* This momentary value, which appears on the face of the stock certificate, has no significance after the first offering.

Preferred Stock, Par Value. The *preferred par value* is often set at $100 so that the fixed annual dividend can be expressed as a percentage of the par: for example, a 5% dividend on a $100 par equals $5 per share annually.

Market Value. The price at which a stock can be bought or sold.

Book Value. This is the *net asset value* of the stock. Subtract the liabilities of a corporation from its assets and divide by the number of shares outstanding and you have the net asset value of the stock.

Rights and Warrants. Rights and warrants are a way for companies to raise capital by giving the current stockholders an opportunity to subscribe to the new shares. Usually rights are short term and warrants are long term. Only one rights issue may be offered at a time. However, many warrant issues may be outstanding at a time.

- *Rights.* A *right,* or *subscription right,* gives current stockholders the privilege to purchase additional shares in proportion to the shares they have. Often this subscription price is lower than the market price. Depending on the number of shares outstanding, a certain number of rights are necessary to purchase one new share. A stockholder may choose to sell his/her rights rather than use them to acquire the new stock. Between the time the stockholders are notified and the issuance of the rights, the stock is sold *cum* (with) rights.

- *Warrants. Warrants* generally come to the market as part of a unit. The holder is entitled to convert the warrant into common stock or some other instrument at a set price within a specific period of time. The parts of the unit can be separated and sold individually.

    Example: A company may issue a $1,000 bond with a warrant to purchase 10 shares of stock.

NOTES:

Figure 14-1. Typical Stock Certificate.

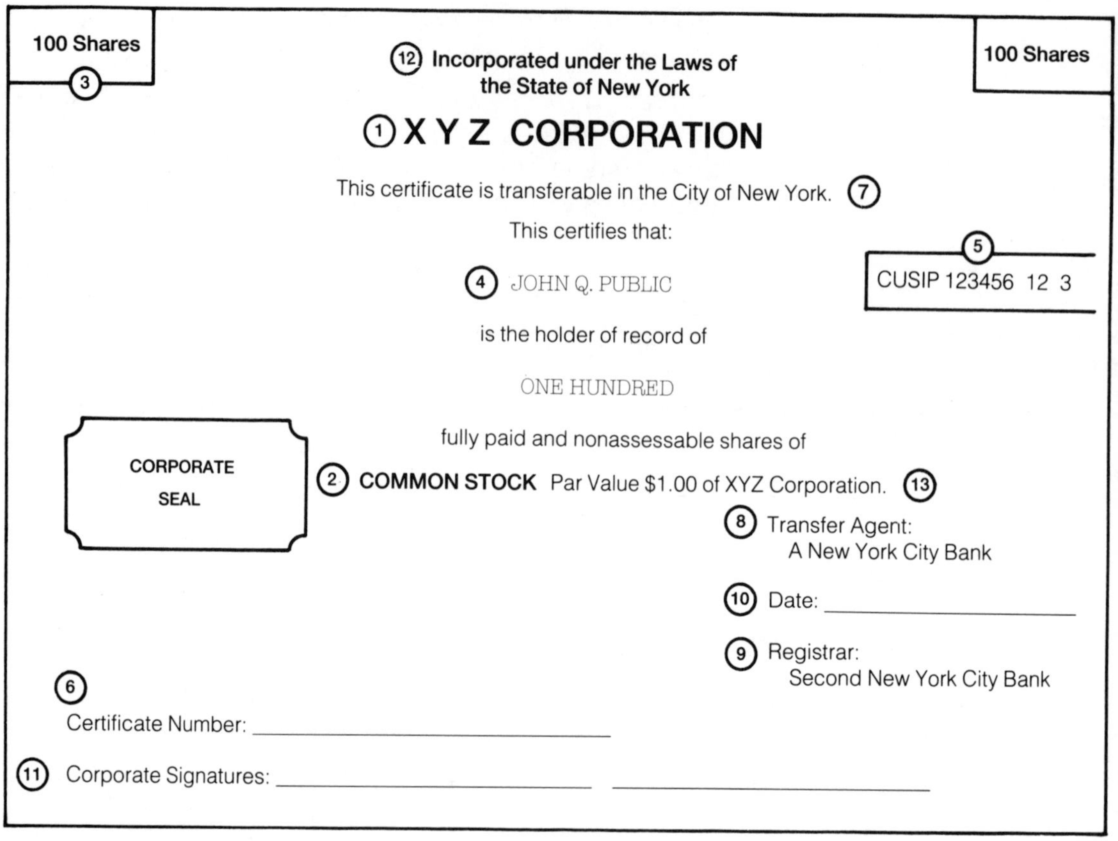

1   Name of corporation

2   Type of stock certificate

3   Number of shares represented by the certificate

4   Name of the registered holder

5   CUSIP—Committee Uniform Security Identification Procedures

6   Certificate number registered with the transfer agent

7   Cities where the certificate may be transferred

8   Transfer agent, usually a bank, is responsible for transferring certificates from seller to buyer, keeping records of all registered shareholders — address, number of shares, sending dividends. The New York Stock Exchange (NYSE) requires all securities traded with them to have a transfer agent in New York City.

9   Registrar is responsible for making sure that the new number of shares equals the old. The NYSE requires that the transfer agent and the registrar be two different banks.

10   Date the certificate is registered with the transfer agent.

11   Authorized corporate officer's signature.

12   The state of incorporation of the company.

13   Par value, the *face value* — an arbitrary issuance value.

Types of Bonds

Corporate bonds. For long-term borrowing of capital involving significant sums of money, corporations turn to debt financing through an offering of bonds. The bondholders lend their money to the corporation in return for interest payments, usually on a semi-annual basis, and a repayment of their principal at the conclusion of the loan's term.

Both *Bearer Certificates* and *Registered to Principal* bonds used to need the "clipping" of coupons to receive interest payments. As of July 1, 1983, the fully-registered bond form has superceded the coupon form. The registrar maintains the name of the owner, or the nominee. The semiannual interest payments are mailed by the corporation's paying agent.

The bonds must be issued to the public under a *trust indenture.* The terms of a corporate bond are found in the indenture (also known as the *deed of trust*), and printed on the certificate's back. The *trustee* is usually a commercial bank.

Mortgage bonds. These are the most prevalent type of secured corporate bond and are supported by a lien on the corporation's property, usually a plant or office building. The mortgage issue may be *open ended,* meaning that subsequent issues are the same as the original issue, or *closed ended,* meaning that subsequent issues are junior to the original issue in the payment of interest and collateral.

Equipment trust. These bonds are supported by equipment used by the corporation in its everyday operation. This type of bond is common in the transportation industry. The issuing corporation usually appoints a large commercial bank as an independent trustee and follows procedures known as the *Philadelphia Plan.*

Collateral trust. These are backed by the securities of another corporation, perhaps a parent company.

Debenture. This is an *unsecured* debt offering by a corporation. This bond is offered by only the strongest companies because it is secured by the good faith and name of the company and not by any tangible assets. High interest is usual to compensate the creditors for their financial exposure.

Figure 14-2. Summary of Protection Available to Bondholders.

Type of Bond	Protection Available
Mortgage	Pledges real assets—real estate
Equipment Trust	Pledges corporate equipment—rolling stock
Collateral Trust	Securities of another corporation
Debenture	Unsecured—Supported by name of corporation

Features of Bonds.

- *Serial Bonds.* This term is often associated with equipment bonds. These bonds require repayment of a portion of the borrowing each year at a series of maturity dates until the entire debt is retired. This self-liquidating debt arrangement is described as a *serial bond.* Also typical of municipal revenue bonds.

- *Income Bonds.* In the event of bankruptcy and reorganization, creditors may be offered a larger principal amount of higher interest-bearing *income bonds* in exchange for their debt issues. Income bonds are long-term debt obligations that promise to pay interest only when, and if, earned by the corporation. Unpayed interest accrues. The corporation remains in bankruptcy until *agreement-adjustment* is reached with the creditors. This is why these are sometimes called *adjustment bonds*.

- *Sinking Fund Bond.* If the indenture requires the corporation to set aside an annual reserve of capital to retire bonds at maturity, a *sinking fund* is created for that purpose.

- *Convertible Bond.* If the indenture contains provisions for the corporation to call the issue, thus forcing the bondholders to convert into equity or lose the economic advantage of the current market price of the stock, the conversion price must be stated in the indenture.

Municipal Bonds

Municipal bonds, or *munis,* are debt instruments issued by state and local governments to raise capital to finance their projects and other needs. A major advantage to munis is that there are no federal taxes on the interest earned on municipals. For those living in the municipality there are no state or local taxes either.

Most of the trading in municipals takes place at the time of the offering by brokerage firms. They buy these bonds for resale to their customers who want tax-free interest payments. A very strong secondary market exists in the OTC market.

Types of Municipal Bonds.

- *General Obligation Bonds.* These bonds are backed by the taxing power of the municipality. The interest payments and money to pay back the principal comes from general tax revenues.

- *A Limited-Tax Bond.* These are backed by a particular tax, such as a state sales tax.

- *Revenue Bonds.* These bonds are secured by and payed back from the income earned by the particular project for which the bonds were issued (such as an energy plant). Instead of having a large bond issue mature at one time, many serial bonds with staggered maturity dates are issued.

- *TANs, RANs and BANs.* These are short-term instruments that are issued in anticipation of tax revenue and offerings.

Figure 14-3. A Typical Bond Certificate.

Bond Certificate

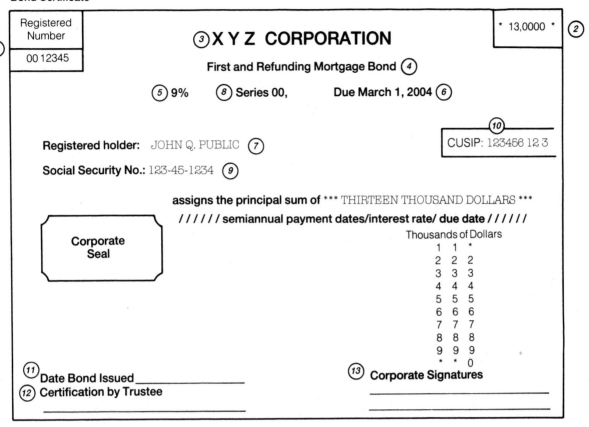

1 Certificate number.

2 Par value in $1,000 increments.

3 Name of corporation.

4 Type of bond.

5 Interest rate.

6 Due date.

7 Name of registered holder.

8 Serial number.

9 Tax identification number of registered owner. Social Security number.

10 CUSIP number — industry identification number.

11 Date bond issued.

12 Certification by trustee.

13 Signature of corporate officers.

Government Securities

Government securities are regarded as the safest investment because they are backed by the full faith and credit and taxing power of the United States Government. The *Federal Reserve Board,* the Fed, issues three types of securities:

1. Treasury bills (T bills)—short-term instruments;
2. Treasury notes (T notes)—intermediate financing; and
3. Treasury bonds (T bonds)—long-term financing.

Treasury Bills. Issued with a maximum maturity of one year with a book-entry form only. Bills are discounted instruments. The difference between the purchase price and the fixed amount at maturity is the discount. The rate of interest earned is built into the discount. It is taxed as ordinary income by the federal government but exempt from state taxation. Minimum denomination is ten thousand plus multiples of five thousand.

Treasury Notes. Issued with a maximum maturity of 10 years. Those notes issued after December 31, 1982 are in book-entry form only. Notes prior to January 1, 1983 are still available in bearer form. They carry a fixed interest rate, paid semiannually, and are issued, quoted, and traded as a percentage of face value. They are non-callable and come in five thousand denominations for maturities of three years or less, and in one thousand denominations for maturities longer than three years.

Treasury Bonds. These are issued with maximum maturity of 30 years. Those bonds issued after September 6, 1982 are in book-entry form only. Bonds prior to January 1, 1983 are still available in bearer form. They carry a fixed interest rate, paid semiannually, and are issued, quoted, and traded as a percentage of face value. It is rarely done but they are callable within five years of the maturity date. These are often referred to as *term bonds.* They may be issued with any maturity date but between five and 35 years is most typical. They can be issued in denominations of $500 to $1 million but $1,000 is the most common.

Flower bonds is a term that is applied to those bonds issued prior to April, 1971 and containing a special provision for the heirs of a bondholder to redeem the bonds at face value, regardless of market value, in satisfaction of federal estate taxes.

Federal Agency Securities

Fannie Maes, Freddie Macs, Ginnie Maes, and Sallie Maes are a family of mortgage-backed securities issued through federal agencies. These securities are not direct obligations of the federal government but do have its sponsorship or guarantee. They are issued by government agencies each of which has been established by an act of Congress.

Federal National Mortgage Association (FNMA) or Fannie Mae. A publicly-owned, government-sponsored corporation which purchases and sells mortgages insured by the Federal Housing Administration (FHA) or Farmers Home Administration (FMHA) or guaranteed by the Veterans Administration (VA). Its funds come from short-term notes, debentures and purchase of its capital stock by approved institutional buyers. Interest on its bonds is fully taxable.

Federal Home Loan Mortgage Corporation or Freddie Mac. The most interesting innovation of this agency was the introduction of the collateralized mortgage obligation (CMO).

Government National Mortgage Association (GNMA) or Ginnie Mae. An offshoot of the FNMA, it is operated by the Department of Housing and Urban Development and offers investors participation in pools of qualified mortgages on private enterprises that are fully guaranteed by the federal government. There are no specific tax exemptions.

- *Pass-through certificates.* Because the monthly interest and partial repayment of principal come from the pooled interest payments of the mortgage holders which are passed through GNMA, the Ginnie Maes are called *pass-through certificates*.
- *TBA GNMA contract, to be announced basis.* These contracts permit GNMA dealers to make a commitment to a specific pool of government-backed mortgages before the certificate is actually issued.
- *Factor table.* This is a way to keep track of the value of the security on a monthly basis. It is necessary because the monthly payments received by the bondholders are part interest and part principal.
- *Trading.* These pass-through securities are traded in the over-the-counter (OTC) market with dealers, brokers, and dealer/brokers in round lots of $1,000,000 or odd lots as low as $25,000.
- *Hedging.* GNMA dealers and traders protect their inventory positions against loss with *puts, calls and future contracts.* For a specified amount of certificates at a set price for a given period a *put* permits its holder to buy, a *call* permits its holder to sell and a futures contract permits its holder to *make or take* delivery of securities.
- *Graduated Payment Mortgage (GPM) and Fixed Payment Mortgage (FPM). Graduated payment mortgages* carry lower initial interest payments gradually increasing with the interest not paid being added to the principal. *Fixed payment mortgages* call for consistent monthly interest payments.

Student Loan Marketing Association (SLMA) or Sallie Mae. Sallie Mae raises capital through periodic offerings of debt obligations and common stock in the company. It promotes two programs:

1. The *Warehouse Advance Program* that makes loans to qualified lending institutions; and

2. The *Loan Purchase Program* that purchases insured student loans from qualified lending institutions. Interest payments are subject to Federal taxes but not state or local taxes. There are restrictions as to who can own the common stock.

Some Other Federal Agency Securities.

- *Banks for Cooperatives* make and service loans for farmer's cooperative associations and issue debt instruments for financing.
- *Federal Land Banks* offer bonds to arrange loans secured by first mortgages on farm or ranch properties for general agricultural purposes. Bonds are backed by participating banks. (Both banks for cooperatives and federal land bank securities have recently been consolidated into a systemwide bond issue.)
- *Federal Home Loan Banks* issues obligations to finance the home building industry in the U.S. by granting mortgage loans.
- *Federal Intermediate Credit Banks* issues debt obligations maturing in five years to make loans to agricultural credit corporations and production associations.
- *Tennessee Valley Authority* obligations are authorized by Congress to promote economic development of the Tennessee River area.
- *U.S. Postal Service.* Since its reorganization as an independent entity in 1971, it has been authorized to issue debt securities to finance capital expenditures and conduct postal operations.

QUIZ 14:1
Securities Explained

Instructions: Enter your responses in the appropriate spaces.

1. Name three types of securities:

_____

_____

_____

Which of these securities has voting rights?

_____

In what order are these securities paid dividends/interest?

First _____

Second _____

Third _____

2. Which type of preferred gives more protection to dividends—cumulative or noncumulative? _____

Why? _____

3. When the preferred is _____, the corporation can retire the stock before the _____.

4. Stocks that are reacquired by a corporation through purchase are called _____ stocks.

5. When current stockholders are given the privilege to purchase additional shares at a subscription price, it is called a

_____.

6. As part of an offering the owner is given the privilege of converting a _____ into common stock at a set price within a specified period of time.

7. Which is the usual form of a bond today: Coupon form? Fully registered form? _____

8. For these four types of bonds, what is pledged to support the bond?

Mortgage _____

Collateral Trust _____

Equipment Trust _____

Debenture _____

9. A self-liquidating debt arrangement is described as a

_____

10. In the event of bankruptcy and reorganization, creditors may be offered an _____.

11. When a corporation sets aside an annual reserve of capital to retire bonds at maturity, it is described as a

_____.

12. Bonds that permit the corporation to call the issue giving the bondholders the option of acquiring common stock at a predetermined price are called _____.

13. Name two types of municipal bonds:

_____

_____

14. Name three types of government securities:

_____

_____

_____

Give the maximum maturity of each security:

_____

_____

_____

15. List the two sources of funds for Fannie Mae:

_____

_____

16. Ginnie Mae offers investors a participation in pools of

_____ on _____.

17. Sallie Mae raises capital through debt obligations and common stock to support which program?

_____

18. Because interest payments for Ginnie Maes come from the pooled interest payments of the mortgage holders, the certificates are described as _____.

19. GNMA traders hedge their inventory positions with:

_____

_____

_____

QUIZ ANSWERS 14:1

Securities Explained

1. Name three types of securities: <u>Common Stock, Preferred Stock, Bonds.</u>
   Which of these securities has voting rights? <u>Common Stock.</u>
   In what order are these securities paid dividends/interest? <u>First Bonds, Second Preferred Stock, Third Common Stock.</u>

2. Which type of preferred gives more protection to dividends—cumulative or noncumulative? <u>Cumulative</u>
   Why? <u>Interest is accumulated when a payment is missed.</u>

3. When the preferred is callable, the corporation can retire the stock before the <u>maturity date.</u>

4. Stocks that are reacquired by a corporation through purchase are called <u>treasury</u> stocks.

5. When current stockholders are given the privilege to purchase additional shares at a subscription price, it is called a <u>right.</u>

6. As part of an offering the owner is given the privilege of converting a <u>warrant</u> into common stock at a set price within a specified period of time.

7. Which is the usual form of a bond today: Coupon form? Fully registered form? <u>Fully registered form.</u>

8. For these four types of bonds, what is pledged to support the bond?

Mortgage	<u>Real Assets</u>
Collateral Trust	<u>Portfolio of securities</u>
Equipment Trust	<u>Production equipment</u>
Debenture	<u>Name of the corporation</u>

9. A self-liquidating debt arrangement is described as a <u>serial bond.</u>

10. In the event of bankruptcy and reorganization, creditors may be offered an <u>income (adjustment) bond.</u>

11. When a corporation sets aside an annual reserve of capital to retire bonds at maturity, it is described as a <u>sinking fund.</u>

12. Bonds that permit the corporation to call the issue giving the bondholders the option of acquiring common stock at a predetermined price are called <u>convertible bonds.</u>

13. Name two types of municipal bonds: <u>General obligation bond, Revenue bond.</u>

14. Name three types of government securities: <u>Treasury bills, Treasury notes, Treasury bonds.</u>
    Give the maximum maturity of each security: <u>One year, Ten years, Thirty years.</u>

15. List the two sources of funds for Fannie Mae: <u>Debt obligations, Stock offering.</u>

16. Ginnie Mae offers investors a participation in pools of <u>qualified mortgages</u> on private enterprises.

17. Sallie Mae raises capital through debt obligations and common stock to support which program? <u>student loan program</u>

18. Because interest payments for Ginnie Maes come from the pooled interest payments of the mortgage holders, the certificates are described as <u>pass-through.</u>

19. GNMA traders hedge their inventory positions with:
    <u>Puts</u>
    <u>Calls</u>
    <u>Futures Contracts</u>

EXERCISE 14:1
Stock Certificate

```
┌──────────────────────────────────────────────────────────────────────┐
│ ┌─────────────┐                                      ┌───────────────┐ │
│ │ 100 Shares  │    Incorporated under the Laws of    │  100 Shares   │ │
│ │     ③       │        the State of New York         │               │ │
│ └─────────────┘                                      └───────────────┘ │
│                    ① X Y Z  CORPORATION                                │
│                                                                        │
│          This certificate is transferable in the City of New York.  ⑦ │
│                         This certifies that:          ┌──────────────┐ │
│                                                    ⑤  │              │ │
│                     ④  JOHN Q. PUBLIC                  │CUSIP 123456 12 3│
│                                                       └──────────────┘ │
│                        is the holder of record of                      │
│                                                                        │
│                            ONE HUNDRED                                  │
│                                                                        │
│ ┌─────────────┐      fully paid and nonassessable shares of            │
│ │             │  ② COMMON STOCK Par Value $1.00 of XYZ Corporation. ⑬  │
│ │  CORPORATE  │                        ⑧ Transfer Agent:               │
│ │    SEAL     │                           A New York City Bank         │
│ │             │                        ⑩ Date: _____          │
│ └─────────────┘                        ⑨ Registrar:                    │
│                                           Second New York City Bank    │
│  ⑥                                                                     │
│   Certificate Number: _____                     │
│  ⑪ Corporate Signatures: _____  _____             │
└──────────────────────────────────────────────────────────────────────┘
```

For each of the numbered items on the stock certificate above, either identify it by filling in the numbered blank below *or* answer the question corresponding to the item.

1. _____

2. _____

3. _____

4. _____

5. CUSIP—Stands for what? _____

6. Certificate Number registered with whom? _____

7. Cities for doing what? _____

8. Transfer Agent—
   usually who? _____
   responsible for what? _____
   _____
   NYSE requirements? _____
   _____

9. Registrar

responsible for what? _____

_____

NYSE requirements? _____

_____

10. Date certificate is registered with whom? _____

11. _____

12. _____

13. Par value, the "face value"—what is the significance of this dollar value? _____

Receiving Securities

As sales assistant you will be involved in activities which support the cashier function. Before we take a look at your specific responsibilities let's review the function of the branch cashier.

The *branch cashier* receives securities, cash and checks from clients. At most branch offices, these items are "received in" to the clients' accounts with the help of *stock received* or *cash received* forms. At the end of each day, the securities are forwarded to the main office, and cash and checks are deposited at the branch's bank. The cashier then prepares *stock received* and *cash received* forms for the CRT operator who transmits the information to the main cashier's office in the home office. This process is called *stock over the wire* (SOW) and *cash over the wire* (COW).

The cashier also prepares checks for clients. When a client wishes to withdraw funds, the account executive (or sales assistant with account executive approval) prepares a check request which is forwarded to the cashier. The cashier, after verifying that there is sufficient cash in the client's account, draws the check.

The following information will help you perform your duties relative to the receipt of securities in your branch. Let's begin with receiving branch mail.

Securities in the Incoming Mail

Typically, mail received in branches is opened in the cashier department where securities and checks are removed and processed. Because of the value of the items received, the area is restricted to certain individuals. Your account executive will be notified when securities or checks are received for his or her clients.

Negotiable and Non-Negotiable Securities

A non-negotiable security has no value and cannot be used in the settlement of any transaction until work has been done to bring the security to "good deliverable" status. Conversely, a negotiable security is one which has value and can be transferred to a new owner.

Certain factors make securities non-negotiable. For example, the stock certificate may be unsigned, or not registered in the same name as the account title, or registered in the name of a deceased person. If the securities are not negotiable, they cannot be deposited in the client's account until the proper documentation is executed to render the certificate negotiable. When non-negotiable securities are received in the mail, they can be held for a few days while the proper documents are completed. If the completion of the proper documents will take more than a few days, the securities must be returned to the client.

In cases where the securities are negotiable and the client's account number is known, the securities are deposited into the client's account.

Personal Delivery of Securities

Sometimes the client will bring in the securities, in which case you will need to:

1. Check the signature(s) on the back of each certificate. Note the signature on the certificate shown below. *The client must sign the certificate exactly as his or her name appears on the front. If the certificate is in the name of more than one party, all parties must sign exactly as their names appear on the front.*

2. Pencil in the account number in the upper right hand corner of each certificate.

3. Give the certificate(s) to the cashier as soon as possible.

4. Ask the client whether he or she would like to go to the cashier to personally pick up a receipt or have it mailed.

A statement of the designations, terms, limitations and relative rights and preferences of the shares of each class authorized to be issued, any variations in relative
rights and preferences between the shares of any series of any class so far as said
rights and preferences shall have been fixed and determined and the authority of
the Board of Directors of the Company to fix and determine any relative rights
and preferences of any subsequent series will be furnished to the holder hereof,
without charge, upon request to the Secretary of the Company or to the Transfer
Agent named on the face hereof.

The following abbreviations, when used in the inscription of ownership on the face of this certificate,
shall be construed as though they were written out in full according to applicable laws or regulations:

          JT TEN   —As joint tenants, with right of
                                survivorship, and not as tenants
                                in common
        TEN IN COM—As tenants in common
        TEN BY ENT—As tenants by the entireties
      Abbreviations in addition to those appearing above may be used.

For value received, _____ *hereby sell, assign and transfer unto*

**PLEASE INSERT SOCIAL SECURITY OR OTHER
IDENTIFYING NUMBER OF ASSIGNEE**

_____
             (PLEASE PRINT OR TYPEWRITE NAME AND ADDRESS OF ASSIGNEE)

_____

_____

_____ *shares*

*of the capital stock represented by the within Certificate,
and do hereby irrevocably constitute and appoint*

_____ *Attorney*

*to transfer the said stock on the books of the within named
Company with full power of substitution in the premises.*

Dated _____

NOTICE: The signature to this assignment must correspond with the name as written upon the face of the certificate in every particular, without alteration or enlargement or any change whatever

Figure 15-1. Illustration of back of stock certificate.

Stock or Bond Power Form

The *stock or bond power form* can be used to render an unsigned certificate negotiable. For example, client John Jones, who lives 30 miles from your branch, has ordered the sale of 100 shares of EFG and he wants the proceeds of the sale mailed to him in the form of a check. Your firm has been holding Mr. Jones' certificate in its vault. Rather than risk loss or damage by mailing the certificate to Mr. Jones for signature, a stock or bond power form is sent instead.

QUIZ 15:1
Receiving Securities

For each of the following items, fill in the blank with the most appropriate response.

1. The person in your branch responsible for preparing checks for clients is the _____.

2. Typically, mail received in branches is opened by the _____.

3. A _____ security has no value and cannot be used in the settlement of a transaction until it is converted to "good deliverable" status.

4. A _____ security has value and can be transferred to a new owner.

5. Two factors that would render a security non-negotiable are:

a. _____

b. _____

For each of the following items, enter a T if the statement is true or an F if the statement is false.

6. _____ It is permissible to deposit negotiable securities into a client's account even if his/her account number is unknown.

7. _____ The signature(s) on the back of a stock certificate must match the name(s) on the front if the certificate is to be negotiable.

8. _____ The account number should be typed into the upper right hand corner of each certificate.

9. _____ If a client wants a receipt for his/her certificate the sales assistant should personally get it from the cashier.

10. _____ A signed stock or bond power form can be used to render an unsigned stock certificate negotiable.

QUIZ ANSWERS 15:1

Receiving Securities

1. The person in your branch responsible for preparing checks for clients is the
    <u>cashier</u>.
2. Typically, mail received in branches is opened by the <u>cashier</u>.
3. A <u>non-negotiable</u> security has no value and cannot be used in the settlement
    of a transaction until it is converted to "good deliverable" status.
4. A <u>negotiable</u> security has value and can be transferred to a new owner.
5. Two factors that would render a security non-negotiable are:
    a. <u>it is unsigned</u>
    b. <u>it is not registered in the same name as the account title</u>

For each of the following items, enter a T if the statement is true or an F if the
statement is false.

6. <u>F</u> It is permissible to deposit negotiable securities into a client's account
    even if his/her account number is unknown.
7. <u>T</u> The signature(s) on the back of a stock certificate must match the
    name(s) on the front if the certificate is to be negotiable.
8. <u>F</u> The account number should be typed into the upper right hand corner of
    each certificate.
9. <u>F</u> If a client wants a receipt for his/her certificate the sales assistant should
    personally get it from the cashier.
10. <u>T</u> A signed stock or bond power form can be used to render an unsigned
    stock certificate negotiable.

**EXERCISE 15:1
Receiving Securities**

See your operations manager or your account executive for answers to the following questions on receiving securities in your branch. Enter the appropriate information in the space provided.

Regarding the receipt of securities in our branch, what procedures (if any) should I follow in each of these areas:

Handling mailed-in securities and checks

_____

_____

_____

_____

_____

_____

_____

Determining whether a security is negotiable or non-negotiable (Be sure to list the criteria used.)

_____

_____

_____

_____

_____

_____

_____

Handling documentation needed to render a non-negotiable security negotiable (Be sure to collect all forms needed, record their names and form numbers below, and insert them in this book.)

_____

_____

_____

_____

_____

_____

_____

_____

Receiving Checks

It is likely that most of your branch's clients will mail in their checks. However, some clients will come into the branch to personally deposit them. Here are some typical guidelines for handling checks. (An upcoming exercise will help you to identify the exact procedures used in your branch.)

1. When receiving a check directly from the client, write the client's account number on the top of the check and take it to the cashier. (If the client needs a receipt he or she will have to personally get it from the cashier.)

2. Checks deposited after the "deposit cut-off time" will go into the next day's bank deposit and it will not be credited to the client's account until the next day. (You will learn your branch's cut-off time in the upcoming exercise.)

3. Checks drawn on an individual's bank account made payable to your firm should only be credited to the account for which the check was drawn. For example, a check drawn on a bank account of Mary Brown payable to your firm should only be credited to the account of *Mary Brown*. Deposit of an individual's check is permitted into a joint account where one of the names on the account is the same as on the check.

4. Checks drawn against corporate or partnership accounts made payable to your firm should only be credited to the corporate account. For example, a check drawn against the ZAP Corporation made payable to your firm should only be credited to the account of ZAP Corporation and not the account of Malcolm Powers, President.

5. Checks drawn on a sole proprietorship for deposit into an individual account may be accepted *only* if a document giving authorization is on file.

6. Third party checks are discouraged.

Time Needed for Checks to Clear

Usually it takes up to eight business days for personal checks to clear. However, the location and size of the paying bank are factors which can delay check clearance for over eight business days. Keep in mind that no withdrawals may be made against these funds until they clear.

Returned Items

Commonly known as *bounced checks,* returned items need to be replaced with *good funds* usually within 48 hours. By good funds we mean monies for which the firm obtains instant credit. Such monies include certified or cashier's checks and cash (U.S. currency only). Because holding cash in the branch office poses a security problem, clients should be encouraged to obtain cashier's checks from their banks for deposit.

Checks Paid to Clients

Proceeds from the sale of securities will be paid automatically on the settlement date if the account executive has coded the order ticket accordingly. If the client wants to be paid by check rather than leave the proceeds of the sale in his account, a *check request form* should be prepared and given to the cashier. Upon receipt of the request the cashier will prepare a check to be mailed to the client. If the client is in the office waiting for the check or will come in to pick it up, notify the cashier when you present the check payout request.

If for any reason funds cannot be paid out, your account executive will be notified. Keep in mind that a client who comes in to pick up a check must go to the cashier and sign for the check. A check cannot be delivered to the client by an employee unless the branch manager approves the exception. (An exercise which follows the quiz on the next page will help you identify the exact procedures for handling checks in your branch.)

QUIZ 15:2
Receiving Securities

For each of the following items, enter a T if the statement is true or an F if the statement is false.

1. _____ When taking a check from a client, the client's account number should be written on the check before it is given to the cashier.

2. _____ If it is known that John Brown is Mary Brown's husband, it is okay to take a check drawn on the account of Mary Brown payable to your firm and credit the account of John Brown.

3. _____ If the president of LMN Corporation asks that a check drawn against LMN Corporation made payable to your firm be credited to his personal account, the president's request should be denied.

4. _____ It usually takes up to eight business days for a personal check to clear.

5. _____ No withdrawals can be made against a personal check deposit until the deposit is cleared.

For each of the following items, fill in the blank with the most appropriate response.

6. Monies for which the firm obtains instant credit are called _____ funds.

7. If a client "bounces" a check he/she should promptly replace it with a _____ check.

8. Usually proceeds from the sale of a security are paid automatically on the _____ date.

9. A client who comes in to pick up a check should get it directly from the _____ .

10. If funds cannot be paid out to a client, the _____ will be notified by the cashier.

QUIZ ANSWERS 15:2

Receiving Securities

1. <u>T</u> When taking a check from a client, the client's account number should be written on the check before it is given to the cashier.

2. <u>F</u> If it is known that John Brown is Mary Brown's husband, it is okay to take a check drawn on the account of Mary Brown payable to your firm and credit the account of John Brown.

3. <u>T</u> If the president of LMN Corporation asks that a check drawn against LMN Corporation made payable to your firm be credited to his personal account, the president's request should be denied.

4. <u>T</u> It usually takes up to eight business days for a personal check to clear.

5. <u>T</u> No withdrawals can be made against a personal check deposit until the deposit is cleared.

For each of the following items, fill in the blank with the most appropriate response.

6. Monies for which the firm obtains instant credit are called <u>good</u> funds.

7. If a client "bounces" a check he/she should promptly replace it with a <u>cashier's</u> check.

8. Usually proceeds from the sale of a security are paid automatically on the <u>settlement</u> date.

9. A client who comes in to pick up a check should get it directly from the <u>cashier.</u>

10. If funds cannot be paid out to a client, the <u>account executive</u> will be notified by the cashier.

EXERCISE 15:2
Receiving Securities

Handling Checks

See your operations manager or your account executive for answers to the following questions on handling checks in your branch.

Regarding the handling of checks in our branch, what procedures (if any) should I be familiar with in each of these areas:

Receiving checks directly from clients:

_____

_____

_____

Our branch's deposit cut-off time is: _____

The use of all related forms such as authorization to transfer funds from a sole proprietorship account to a personal account, check request form, etc. (Be sure to collect all forms needed, record their names and form numbers below, and insert them into this section of your book.)

_____

_____

_____

_____

Handling returned items:

_____

_____

_____

_____

Requesting checks from the cashier:

_____

_____

_____

_____

Automatic Dividend Accounts

Stocks pay dividends when declared by a corporate board of directors. Dividends may be in cash or stock and they are issued on a per-share basis to all registered owners of the stock on a specific date. Many firms have *automatic dividend accounts* which pay out accumulated dividends and interest to clients on a monthly basis. However, each firm has its own methods and procedures relative to the payment of dividends. Please complete the exercise on the following page so you will understand your branch's system of dividend payment.

EXERCISE 15:3
Receiving Securities

Automatic Dividend Account Procedure

See your operations manager or account executive for answers to the following questions regarding your branch's system for the payment of dividends to its clients.

What does our system for the payment of dividends to clients consist of?

_____

_____

_____

_____

_____

_____

_____

_____

How often are payments made and on what date(s)?

_____

_____

What is the minimum amount per check? The maximum?

_____

Where are the checks mailed out?

_____

What do the checks look like? (Photocopy a sample and insert it into this section of your book.)

What are my responsibilities relative to the payment of dividends? How do I carry them out?

_____

_____

_____

_____

_____

_____

_____

_____

Transfer of Customer Securities

Sometimes clients with cash accounts prefer to hold their securities (certificates) rather than leave them on deposit with the firm. The client's request to receive the securities can be made either automatically or manually. Typically the automatic request is made by simply entering a code on the order ticket, which will automatically put the security into transfer. A request to transfer and ship can also be accomplished manually by completing an instruction request form which is given to the branch operations area.

The following exercise will help familiarize you with the procedures and forms used to transfer securities in your branch.

EXERCISE 15:4
Receiving Securities

Transfer of Securities

See your operations manager or account executive for answers to the following questions on transferring securities in your branch.

Would you explain the automatic system we use to transfer customer securities?

_____

_____

_____

_____

_____

_____

_____

_____

_____

What are my responsibilities relative to the automatic system? (Be sure to collect all forms needed, record the names and form numbers below, and insert them into this section of your book.)

_____

_____

_____

_____

_____

_____

_____

_____

_____

Would you explain the manual system we use to transfer customer securities?

_____

_____

_____

_____

_____

_____

_____

_____

_____

_____

What are my responsibilities relative to the manual system? (Be sure to collect all forms needed, record their names and form numbers below, and insert them into this section of your book.)

_____

_____

_____

_____

_____

_____

_____

_____

_____

_____

Mutual Funds

Many firms offer a number of mutual funds for investment under headings such as *aggressive growth, tax-free municipals, government agencies,* and so on. Such funds give clients two options:

1. the option of investing in a pool of professionally managed securities rather than one particular security (the advantage to clients is minimized risk through diversification); and

2. the option of an interest-generating *parking space* for their money while they decide on what to invest in next.

For the sales assistant, the challenge of mutual funds is in helping the account executive maintain a system to manage such funds.

Goals of the Mutual Funds System

A mutual funds system should include methods for:

1. Keeping track of client credit balances that should be invested. (For example, sales of securities will result in a credit balance on the settlement date. These funds should be sent to the client or immediately invested in a mutual fund operated by the firm.)

2. Investing money into the funds. (Typically an order ticket must be filled out by the account executive.)

The procedures to attain these two broad goals are unique to each branch. Consequently an exercise that will pinpoint the mutual funds procedures for your branch follows.

See your account executive for answers to the following questions regarding your branch's mutual funds system.

What mutual funds do we offer? (Be sure to get all brochures and forms needed, record the names and publication numbers below, and insert them into this section of your book.)

_____

_____

_____

_____

_____

_____

_____

_____

_____

_____

How can we determine when a client has money to invest into one of our mutual funds?

_____

_____

_____

_____

_____

_____

_____

_____

_____

_____

_____

What type of order ticket do you use to invest the client's money? (Get a photocopy of a completed order ticket and insert it in this section of your book. Be sure that you understand the order ticket's content. There is space below for notes.)

_____

_____

_____

_____

_____

When are dividends paid and how are they reported to the client?
(Get a photocopy of a client's monthly statement which includes a
mutual fund investment and review it with your account executive.
Be sure to note below all pertinent information you will need to
answer client questions about their statements. Insert the photocopy into this section for future reference.)

_____

_____

_____

_____

_____

_____

_____

_____

_____

*Would you explain the step-by-step operation of our branch's
mutual fund system and my responsibilities for each step?*

_____

_____

_____

_____

_____

_____

_____

_____

_____

_____

_____

_____

_____

_____

_____

_____

_____

_____

Lost Certificate Procedure

The following is a review of the procedure for transferring securities so that you are reminded of the procedure. If these procedures are followed, the amount of lost certificates should be greatly reduced. If a certificate becomes lost, the *lost certificate procedure* on page 210 should help.

- *Request.* The order to transfer a specific security is given to branch operations.
- *Transfer.* The home office forwards the request to the transfer agent bank. Both the bank and the cities in which the certificate can be transferred are listed on the face of the security.
- *Record.* NYSE rules require that the registrar bank be a different bank than the transfer agent bank. The certificate of ownership is recorded by the registrar bank and the client's name is then imprinted on the certificate.
- *Review.* The certificate is returned to the firm's home office for review before being mailed to the client.
- *Tracking.* Forms are completed to document the delivery details: an affidavit of mailing, a stock/bond power, and the client statement.
- *Timing.* It can take as long as two weeks before the certificate is received by the client. Keep this in mind when responding to client inquiries.

"Where's my Certificate?": The Lost Certificate Procedure

Client Responsibilities

Not all clients want the actual physical certificate in their possession. For those who do, it is their responsibility to look at their monthly statement for the dated-delivery entry, and to report non-delivery to the branch within 90 days.

The Firm's Responsibilities

If the non-delivery is reported within 90 days, the firm will replace the lost document.

Your job is to:

1. check with the home office operations to make sure the certificate has not been returned to them and credited to the client's account;

2. provide operations with a description of the security, the quantity to be delivered, and the delivery method;

3. obtain from the AE a copy of the client's statement and check it for the delivery entry;

4. request a *mail loss affidavit* and a stock/bond power from operations (mail these forms to the client for their notarized signatures);

5. when the signed and notarized forms have been returned, give them to operations for processing; and

6. notify the client that it will take four to six weeks to replace the missing certificate.

Note: If after receiving a certificate the client loses it, the firm usually cannot replace the certificate for the client. The client must deal directly with the transfer agent.

Check with your operations manager for the exact procedure to be used in your branch and obtain copies of the applicable forms for inclusion in this workbook.

NOTE the exact procedure for your branch:

_____

_____

_____

_____

_____

_____

QUIZ 17:1
Lost Certificate Procedures

Instructions: Enter your responses in the appropriate spaces.

1. Clients who want to get the certificates should check their
   _____ _____ for a dated delivery entry.

2. Clients have _____ days to report nondelivery.

3. Clients may have to be reminded that it takes a minimum of
   _____ weeks before delivery can be made.

4. Before assuming that the certificate was lost, you must check
   with the home office to make sure the certificate was not
   _____ and _____ to the client's ac-
   count.

5. The two forms that you need to get a new certificate are:

   _____

   _____

6. The client must sign and _____ these forms.

7. It takes _____ to _____ weeks to re-
   place the missing certificates once you get the completed
   forms back.

QUIZ ANSWERS 17:1

Lost Certificate Procedures

1. Clients who want to get the certificates should check their <u>monthly statement</u> for a dated delivery entry.
2. Clients have <u>90</u> days to report nondelivery.
3. Clients may have to be reminded that it takes a minimum of <u>two</u> weeks before delivery can be made.
4. Before assuming that the certificate was lost, you must check with the home office to make sure the certificate was not <u>returned</u> and <u>credited</u> to the client's account.
5. The two forms that you need to get a new certificate are:
   <u>mail loss affidavit</u>
   <u>stock bond power</u>
6. The client must sign and <u>notarize</u> these forms.
7. It takes <u>four</u> to <u>six</u> weeks to replace the missing certificates once you get the completed forms back.

Branch Collections

Settlement Terminology

Jill Jones has a cash account with Smith and Smith. She called her account executive, Jim Brown, on Wednesday to buy 100 shares of XYZ Corp. This is the *trade date*. She knows that she has to pay within five business days.

This means that the following Wednesday would be her *settlement date* for this buy. She expected to pay with a bonus from her job. The check she was promised did not arrive. On the day after the settlement date, her account executive got a *six-day wire notice* that the payment had not come into the branch. Jim Brown called Jill immediately to arrange for the payment. She told Jim about her bonus and said that if it hadn't gotten to her in a few days she would take money from her money market account for the shares.

Jim told his sales assistant to return the notice to the cage with an indication that payment would be coming in later that week. This triggered the firm into applying for a *five-day extension.* The payment from Jill had not arrived two days after the extension. A mailgram advising Jill that her account would be sold out on Friday was sent. At that point Jill sent the money.

NOTE any special procedures for your branch:

_____

_____

_____

Figure 18-1. Example of Branch Collections.

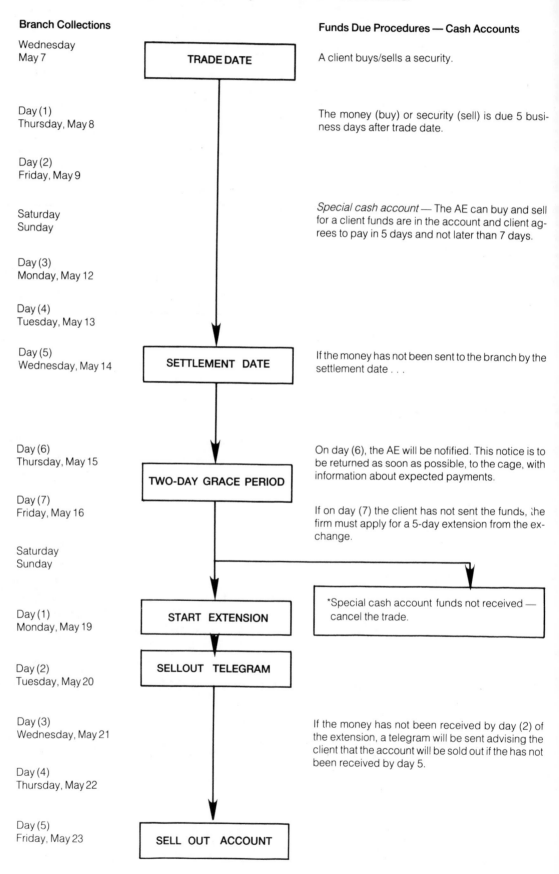

Branch Collections

Wednesday
May 7

Day (1)
Thursday, May 8

Day (2)
Friday, May 9

Saturday
Sunday

Day (3)
Monday, May 12

Day (4)
Tuesday, May 13

Day (5)
Wednesday, May 14

Day (6)
Thursday, May 15

Day (7)
Friday, May 16

Saturday
Sunday

Day (1)
Monday, May 19

Day (2)
Tuesday, May 20

Day (3)
Wednesday, May 21

Day (4)
Thursday, May 22

Day (5)
Friday, May 23

TRADE DATE

SETTLEMENT DATE

TWO-DAY GRACE PERIOD

START EXTENSION

SELLOUT TELEGRAM

SELL OUT ACCOUNT

Funds Due Procedures — Cash Accounts

A client buys/sells a security.

The money (buy) or security (sell) is due 5 business days after trade date.

Special cash account — The AE can buy and sell for a client funds are in the account and client agrees to pay in 5 days and not later than 7 days.

If the money has not been sent to the branch by the settlement date . . .

On day (6), the AE will be nofified. This notice is to be returned as soon as possible, to the cage, with information about expected payments.

If on day (7) the client has not sent the funds, the firm must apply for a 5-day extension from the exchange.

*Special cash account funds not received — cancel the trade.

If the money has not been received by day (2) of the extension, a telegram will be sent advising the client that the account will be sold out if the has not been received by day 5.

Figure 18-2 is an example of a six-day wire. The day after the *settlement date* the account executive will receive a notice, such as this, advising which accounts are past due. The procedure to follow is to return this notice to the cage with information obtained from the client about when they will pay.

NYSE Rule about Extensions

The rule states that five extensions in 12 calendar months is the maximum allowed. After these five extensions, all future trades must be paid for on settlement date or have the account sold out immediately.

Exempt Securities

U.S. government bonds and municipal bonds are not subject to the extension rules. These exempt trades must be settled on the settlement date and all payments must be complete in seven days. The firm must pay out the funds in the case of a buy or take a charge against firm capital for the short securities but should not file for an extension.

FIRST NOTICE to Account Executive of Cash or Securities Due

Acct Exec	Office	T	Customer's Name

On the settlement date ——————————————— this account will owe us the items listed below.

PLEASE CONTACT YOUR CUSTOMER

☐ Federal Call_____   ☐ Stock Power_____

☐ Cash_____   ☐ Other_____

☐ Short Dividend_____   ☐ Securities_____

☐ Maintenance Call_____   ☐ Legal Papers_____

Figure 18-2. Example of a Six-day Wire.

Figure 18-3. Branch Collections.

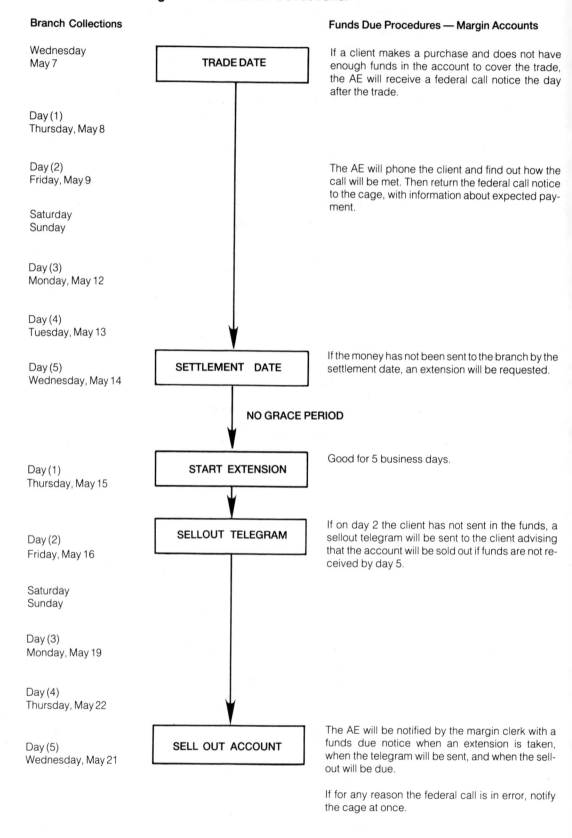

Branch Collections

Wednesday
May 7

Day (1)
Thursday, May 8

Day (2)
Friday, May 9

Saturday
Sunday

Day (3)
Monday, May 12

Day (4)
Tuesday, May 13

Day (5)
Wednesday, May 14

Day (1)
Thursday, May 15

Day (2)
Friday, May 16

Saturday
Sunday

Day (3)
Monday, May 19

Day (4)
Thursday, May 22

Day (5)
Wednesday, May 21

TRADE DATE

SETTLEMENT DATE

NO GRACE PERIOD

START EXTENSION

SELLOUT TELEGRAM

SELL OUT ACCOUNT

Funds Due Procedures — Margin Accounts

If a client makes a purchase and does not have enough funds in the account to cover the trade, the AE will receive a federal call notice the day after the trade.

The AE will phone the client and find out how the call will be met. Then return the federal call notice to the cage, with information about expected payment.

If the money has not been sent to the branch by the settlement date, an extension will be requested.

Good for 5 business days.

If on day 2 the client has not sent in the funds, a sellout telegram will be sent to the client advising that the account will be sold out if funds are not received by day 5.

The AE will be notified by the margin clerk with a funds due notice when an extension is taken, when the telegram will be sent, and when the sellout will be due.

If for any reason the federal call is in error, notify the cage at once.

Margin

Margin accounts require a great deal of attention from the account executive, the sales assistant and the back office. There are many options for the client, most of which fluctuate with the market. Careful management of these accounts can open sales opportunities for the account executive and money-making positions for the client. Careful management is also necessary to avoid risk, and possible loss, for the firm. Sales assistants must be aware of all of these possibilities and what they can do to aid the account executive and the margin department.

Margin Terminology

Margin (or Credit) Account Department. It is here that the firm places the responsibility to monitor the current status of each customer's margin account. They act as the firms *watchdogs* to maintain these accounts in conformance with the rules and regulations of the Securities and Exchange Commission.

Regulation T. This is the Federal Reserve Board regulation that governs margin accounts. The NYSE and NASD enforce and augment it. For instance: Rules 431-432 of the New York Stock Exchange cover minimum equity requirements and minimum maintenance requirements.

Marginable Securities. Typically all securities on the national exchanges, and those OTC securities that have been approved by the Federal Reserve Board, are marginable. However each firm has the final say on which securities it permits its customers to purchase on margin and which customers qualify for margin accounts.

Federal Calls. Joe Bell places an order to buy a security on margin. If there are insufficient funds to cover the trade the firm's margin department will send a *Federal call notice* to the account executive the day after the trade. The AE will call the client to find when the necessary funds will be sent in. This Federal Call Notice must be returned to the cage with information about when funds can be expected.

Example: Check in mail 5-12 // LMN FM Type 1 //

If the funds are not received by the settlement date, the firm must apply for an extension from an appropriate self-regulatory organization such as the NYSE, AMEX, PCE, PHLX, or NASD.

Close-Outs. If the request is turned down, the firm has to close-out the transaction. If the client does not send in the funds, a sellout mailgram must be sent. It will advise the client that the account will be sold out on the final date of the extension if the funds are not received.

NOTE any special procedures for your branch:

_____

_____

_____

_____

_____

_____

Market Value. This is the price at which a security can be purchased.

Margin Rate. This determines the minimum the client must pay or deposit against a transaction. The rate is fixed by the Federal Reserve Board. It is expressed as a percentage.

Loan Value. The amount clients can borrow from the firm to purchase certain securities is called the *loan value.*

Debit Balance. This is the interest bearing loan the firm makes to a client in order to purchase a security.

Equity. The difference between the debit balance and the market value.

Equity $ + Debit Balance $ = Current Market Value

NOTE any special margin rules for your firm:

_____

_____

_____

_____

_____

Excess and Buying Power. This expresses the increased options a client gets when a security appreciates in value. It can be used to buy more stock. The firm can lend the difference to the client. Or the client may withdraw the excess.

Maintenance Call. This happens when the value of an account falls and the brokerage firm must "call" for additional money.

House Calls. In this case, the *minimum maintenance requirement rules* must be enforced. The rule states that when the equity goes below one-third of the debit balance, firms must send a "call" to a client for additional money, or equity, to be deposited. Typically the client has 72 hours to meet this call. If the client does not meet the needs of the call, the firm must liquidate enough securities to satisfy this requirement. The firm must sell three and one-third times the amount of the call to meet a house call. House call requirements are based on the firm's policy.

NOTE any special rules for your firm:

_____

_____

_____

_____

_____

_____

NYSE (New York Stock Exchange) Call. These calls are issued when the equity drops below 25 percent of the market value. The client has 48 hours to meet this call. The firm must sell four times the amount of the call to meet a NYSE call. This call is based on NYSE rules.

There is a very brief time between the margin department's notification to the account executive that money is due and the time the client must send in the money. The client must be called immediately.

The notice will indicate when the telegram was sent to the client and when the sellout will be done if the funds are not received. As with other funds due notices, the notice must be returned as soon as possible with information about when the client will send in the funds.

NOTE any special procedures for your branch:

_____

_____

_____

_____

_____

_____

Restricted Accounts. This situation occurs when the account has a debit balance that is higher than the current loan value. Regulation T has these rules to govern this situation:

- when the client decides to purchase new securities, the firm should require margin only for the new purchase but does not have to compel the client to bring the entire account up to margin requirements;
- when a client decides to sell a security from a restricted account only 50 percent of the proceeds can be withdrawn.

Items Due. The credit department is continually informing branch personnel about items that are pending or actual deficiencies in a client's account. Included in item due wires are:

1. Money due on T calls—the funds owed by a client on a transaction.

2. Money due on house calls—the funds owed by a customer to satisfy an equity deficiency.

3. Securities (stocks or bonds)—due to be delivered to the branch by a client against a sale in the account.

4. Any other pending problems.

NOTE any special procedures used in your branch:

_____

_____

_____

_____

_____

_____

THIS PAGE IS FOR A COPY OF
YOUR FIRM'S POLICY ON MARGIN ACCOUNTS
INCLUDING GENERAL GUIDELINES ABOUT:

Margin consent agreement
Minimum initial equity
Interest policies
Credit Manager approvals
  and
Specific Security Guidelines
  - Type of Security
  - Type of Account
  - Initial Margin Required
  - Maintenance Requirements

QUIZ 18:1
Branch Collections

Instructions: Enter your response in the appropriate spaces.

Calendar for September 1986

Sun	Mon	Tues	Wed	Thurs	Fri	Sat
	1	2	3	4	5	6
7	8	9	10	11	12	13
14	15	16	17	18	19	20
21	22	23	24	25	26	27
28	29	30				

1. For a *cash account*—If a client puts in an order to buy a security on Sept. 3:

What would be the settlement date? _____

What date would the AE be notified of nonpayment?

_____

What date would the extension start? _____

What date would a sellout telegram be sent?

_____

What date would the account be closed out?

_____

2. For a *special cash account*—If a client puts in an order to buy a security on Sept. 9:

What would be the last date he/she could pay?

_____

3. For a *margin account*—If a client puts in an order to buy a security on Sept. 11:

What date might the AE get a federal call notice?

_____

What would this federal call indicate?

_____

What would be the settlement date? _____

What date would an extension start? _____

How many days are in this extension period? _____

4. How many extensions does the NYSE allow per year?

_____

5. What security purchases disallow extensions?

_____

_____

6. What is the Federal Reserve Board regulation that covers margin accounts? _____

7. Tom Ivy calls his account executive and places an order for 100 shares of GTF at $60 to be bought using his margin account. He pays $3,000 cash for the GTF stock.

   What is the market value of GTF? _____

   What is the margin rate? _____

   How much is the debit balance? _____

   How much equity does Tom have in GTF? _____

8. If GTF went down in price so that Tom's equity in it was less then one-third of the debit balance, a _____
   _____would be triggered. The client has _____ hours to meet this call.

9. If GTF went down in price so that Tom's equity in it was less than one-quarter of the _____ _____, a NYSE call would be triggered. The client has _____ hours to meet this call.

10. If Tom bought 100 shares of ABC at $50/share with a 60% margin

    How much cash would he pay? $_____

    What would be the debit balance? $_____

    What would be the loan value? $_____

    What would be the equity? $_____

NOTES:

QUIZ ANSWERS 18:1
Branch Collections
Calendar for September 1986

Sun	Mon	Tues	Wed	Thurs	Fri	Sat
	1	2	3	4	5	6
7	8	9	10	11	12	13
14	15	16	17	18	19	20
21	22	23	24	25	26	27
28	29	30				

1. For a *cash account*—If a client puts in an order to buy a security on Sept. 3:
   What would be the settlement date? Sept. 10
   What date would the AE be notified of nonpayment? Sept. 11
   What date would the extension start? Sept. 15
   What date would a sellout telegram be sent? Sept. 16
   What date would the account be closed out? Sept. 19

2. For a *special cash account*—If a client puts in an order to buy a security on Sept. 9:
   What would be the last date he/she could pay? Sept. 12

3. For a *margin account*—If a client puts in an order to buy a security on Sept. 11:
   What date might the AE get a federal call notice? Sept. 12
   What would this federal call indicate?
   Insufficient cash in the account to cover the trade.
   What would be the settlement date? Sept. 17
   What date would an extension start? Sept. 18
   How many days are in this extension period? 5 days

4. How many extensions does the NYSE allow per year? five

5. What security purchases disallow extensions?
   U.S. government bonds
   Municipal bonds

6. What is the Federal Reserve Board regulation that covers margin accounts?
   Regulation T

7. Tom Ivy calls his account executive and places an order for 100 shares of GTF at $60 to be bought using his margin account. He pays $3,000 cash for the GTF stock.
   What is the market value of GTF? $60
   What is the margin rate? 50%
   How much is the debit balance? $3,000
   How much equity does Tom have in GTF? $3,000

8. If GTF went down in price so that Tom's equity in it was less then one-third of the debit balance, a house call would be triggered. The client has 72 hours to meet this call.

9. If GTF went down in price so that Tom's equity in it was less than one-quarter of the market value a NYSE call would be triggered. The client has 48 hours to meet this call.

10. If Tom bought 100 shares of ABC at $50/share with a 60% margin
    How much cash would he pay? $3,000
    What would be the debit balance? $2,000
    What would be the loan value? $2,000
    What would be the equity? $3,000

Dividends

Dividends are payments made to shareholders of securities. They may be paid out by check or reinvested to purchase more securities. As you would expect, efficiency in handling dividends is vital to good client relations. Furthermore, delays or errors in filing dividend claims may result in a direct loss to the firm. We will cover your role relative to dividends, but first some background on this important area is in order.

An Overview of Dividends

Stocks pay dividends when declared by a corporate board of directors. *Dividends*, which are payments, may be in cash or stock. They are issued on a per-share basis to all registered owners of the stock on a specific date. Whether a corporation pays a dividend, or decides to omit a dividend, depends on the policy, plans and current financial condition of the company.

Three important dates affect the dividend cycle: the *ex-dividend, record*, and *payable* dates. The corporation sets these dates for each dividend.

- The *ex-dividend date* is the date the client must own the stock in order to participate in the distribution. If the stock is sold on the ex-dividend date the client will get the dividend. If the client buys on the ex-dividend date he or she is *not* entitled to the dividend. The seller will get it. Consequently, the *trade date* determines who will get the dividend.

- The *record date* is used by the transfer agent to decide who will get the dividend check. If the security is in the client's name, the agent will mail a dividend check directly to the client. If the security is in the name of the firm, the agent will mail the check to the firm.

- The *payable date* is the date that the client should receive the check directly from the transfer agent or the date the account will be credited if the stock is in the name of the firm.

> *Example:* Using the dates mentioned above, suppose *International Crube & Son* declares the $0.25 per share dividend on April 1 to holders of record Friday, May 1. To receive the dividend, one must be the registered owner of the security on Friday evening, May 1. The last opportunity to purchase the stock and receive the dividend on a *regular-way basis* (five business days) would be the preceding Friday, April 24. A buyer on that day would settle the transaction on May 1 and would thereby become the holder of record. The seller of the security would no longer be entitled to the dividend.
>
> A purchaser of the security on Monday, April 27, however, would not be entitled to the dividend because that transaction would settle Monday, May 4. To account for the $0.25 per share dividend, the market price of the security would be reduced by the amount of the dividend or next highest trading fraction. In the case of a $0.25 dividend, the market price of the stock will ordinarily fall a quarter of a point. A security closing at $40 a share on the day before the ex-date will open at 39¾ on the ex-date.

Sometimes a corporation wants to declare a dividend to its shareholders but wishes to conserve cash. In this case, it may elect to pay a *stock dividend.* Stock dividends are paid as a percentage of outstanding stock. A 10 percent stock dividend would mean a distribution of one new share for every 10 shares a stockholder already owned. The owner of 100 shares, for example, would receive a stock dividend of 10 shares.

It is also noteworthy that transactions in securities undergoing a large stock dividend or stock split must be controlled during the dividend period. As is true of any dividend, the owner of the security on record date is entitled to the dividend. However, transactions in the stock of corporations that have declared stock splits or large stock dividends that settle after the record date but before the payable date will be traded at full price. The value of these securities will decrease on the ex-date, which is the day after the payable date.

An investor in a stock that is due to split or pay a large stock dividend must be protected during this period. This protection is provided by a *due bill,* a legal statement that guarantees to the buyer that additional shares will be delivered on or shortly after the payable date. It is an I.O.U. for stock from seller to buyer. It goes into effect on the trade date, which is four business days before the record date, and "comes off" on the first trade day after payable. If the selling firm settles a transaction before the record date, no due bill is necessary.

If any trade is not settled by the record date, or if the actual settlement date is after the record date but before the payable date, due bills must accompany the delivery. By means of the due bill, the client can buy the "old" stock at the old price and can be assured that the additional shares will be delivered when they are issued. The dividend department keeps records of all due bills issued and received by the company.

A client accustomed to cash dividends may not understand why the price of the stock did not drop on the ex-date of the split. (You must be able to explain that for splits and stock dividends over 25 percent, the ex-date is normally the day after the payable date.) Most times though, clients are interested in when the dividend is going to "hit" (be credited to) their accounts.

A Very Common Problem

Sometimes clients receive dividends that they are not entitled to directly from transfer agents. This usually occurs when stock is sold by the client before the ex-dividend date but the stock remains in the client's name over the record date. Because the client's name is on the books as the owner on the record date, the transfer agent mails the check directly to the client. In such cases, the client must return the check to the firm so payment can be made to the buyer of the stock.

Note: Keep in mind that all information regarding dividends (ex-dividend, record and payable dates) can be found in the *Standard & Poor's Daily Dividend Record.* See Section 11, "Publications."

Your Role in Handling Dividend Problems

As sales assistant you will be assisting clients with dividend problems. When you know the right questions to ask you can efficiently work with branch operations to solve dividend problems and maintain good relations with clients.

The steps listed below outline a good approach to take in researching dividend problems. Later on you will complete an exercise that will produce a detailed outline tailored to your branch's requirements.

Typical Scenario

A client calls complaining that a dividend was not credited to his/her account. *As sales assistant you should:*

1. See if the account is credited. Check the client's monthly statement.

2. Make sure that the client is entitled to the dividend. Check the client's monthly statement to determine if he or she owned the security on the ex-dividend date.

3. Determine if the securities were in transfer over the record date. Furnish operations with the date the security was transferred and shipped.

4. See whether there was an "as of" trade settling after the record date. Provide operations with the correct settlement date and a copy of the "as of" confirmation.

5. See if there was a trade correction affecting dividends. Provide operations with the settlement date of the corrected trade.

6. Determine if exchanges were processed over the ex-date. Give operations the date of the new certificate and its registration number.

7. Look up information in the *Standard & Poor's Dividend Record Book* (check dates).

8. See if it is a split situation. Stock splits are generally not credited to the client's account until several business days to a week after the payable date (the "due bill" period).

9. Write up the information you have researched and give it to the individual who is ultimately responsible for dividend claims in your branch.

Dividends are important to your branch's clients. To keep them satisfied you will need to answer their questions promptly and accurately. Please complete the quiz on dividends and the exercise which follow.

QUIZ 19:1
Dividends

For each of the following items, fill in the blank with the most appropriate response.

1. Define ex-dividend date: _____

_____

2. Define record date: _____

_____

3. Define payable date: _____

_____

4. Define due bill: _____

_____

For each of the following items, enter T if the statement is true or an F if the statement is false.

5. _____ Dividends may be paid out to clients by check or automatically reinvested to purchase more securities.

6. _____ If a client buys on the ex-dividend date he/she is entitled to the dividend.

7. _____ It is permissible for a company to pay a dividend in the form of a percentage of outstanding stock.

8. _____ Transactions in securities undergoing a large stock dividend or stock split are decontrolled during the dividend period.

9. _____ Due bills must accompany the delivery of securities when a trade is not settled by the record date.

10. _____ Due bills need not accompany the delivery of securities when the actual settlement date is after the record date but before the payable date.

11. _____ If a client sells a stock before the ex-dividend date but the stock remains in the client's name over the record date, the client will probably get a dividend check.

12. _____ Stock splits are not credited to the client's account until the seventh business day after the payable date.

QUIZ ANSWERS 19:1

Dividends

1. Define ex-dividend date: <u>the date the client must own the stock in order to participate in the distribution of dividends.</u>
2. Define record date: <u>the date used by the transfer agent to determine who will get the dividend check, i.e., the owner of record on this date gets the check.</u>
3. Define payable date: <u>the date that the client should receive the check directly from the transfer agent or the date the account will be credited if the stock is in the name of the firm.</u>
4. Define due bill: <u>a legal statement or I.O.U. that guarantees to the buyer of a stock that shares will be delivered on or shortly after the payable date in the event of an impending stock split or payment of a large stock dividend.</u>

For each of the following items, enter T if the statement is true or an F if the statement is false.

5. <u>T</u> Dividends may be paid out to clients by check or automatically reinvested to purchase more securities.
6. <u>F</u> If a client buys on the ex-dividend date he/she is entitled to the dividend.
7. <u>T</u> It is permissible for a company to pay a dividend in the form of a percentage of outstanding stock.
8. <u>F</u> Transactions in securities undergoing a large stock dividend or stock split are decontrolled during the dividend period.
9. <u>T</u> Due bills must accompany the delivery of securities when a trade is not settled by the record date.
10. <u>F</u> Due bills need not accompany the delivery of securities when the actual settlement date is after the record date but before the payable date.
11. <u>T</u> If a client sells a stock before the ex-dividend date but the stock remains in the client's name over the record date, the client will probably get a dividend check.
12. <u>T</u> Stock splits are not credited to the client's account until the seventh business day after the payable date.

EXERCISE 19:1
Dividends

See your operations manager for answers to the following questions on dividend procedures in your branch.

Who in our branch has primary responsibility for handling dividend problems?

_____

What are our responsibilities relative to the handling of due bills? (Get a photocopy of a due bill and review its content with the operations manager. Insert the copy in this section of the book.)

_____

_____

_____

_____

_____

_____

_____

_____

_____

What is the procedure for correcting the problem of a dividend check having been mailed to a client who is not entitled to the dividend?

_____

_____

_____

_____

_____

_____

_____

_____

_____

_____

What is the best approach to investigating a client complaint regarding an unpaid dividend? (There should be a separate procedure if complaint is in writing.) (Review the steps shown on page 229 with your operations manager. Ask him or her to point out similarities and differences as you prepare the list of steps pertinent to your branch in the space below. Be sure to collect all relevant forms, review their use and insert them in this section of your book as you proceed from step to step.)

_____

_____

_____

_____

_____

_____

_____

_____

_____

_____

_____

_____

_____

_____

_____

_____

_____

_____

_____

What are my responsibilities relative to the handling of dividends in our branch?

_____

_____

_____

_____

_____

_____

_____

_____

_____

_____

_____

_____

EDP in
the Brokerage Environment

Perhaps there is no business anywhere that is as heavily-computerized as brokerage. A client's main contact with a firm is through an account executive by telephone. But the account executive and everybody else in the firm is connected to the home office—as well as all of the world's markets and the data bases that form the basis for investment decisions—by computers, modems, and satellites.

This entire workbook has been devoted to translating the verbal contact with the client into print forms and documents. If the transaction rate was in the thousands or even in the tens of thousands, people by themselves could probably handle the volume. With the trading volume reaching into the multimillions every day, however, there is no way to handle it all without the computer.

Daily Reports:

- customer trade confirmations;
- P&S trade blotters;
- cashier's receive and deliver blotters;
- the stock record;
- daily cash listing;
- dividend position listing;
- margin status reports;
- "seg" reports;
- inventory positions.

Figure 20-1. Overview of Electronic Data Processing in the Brokerage Environment.

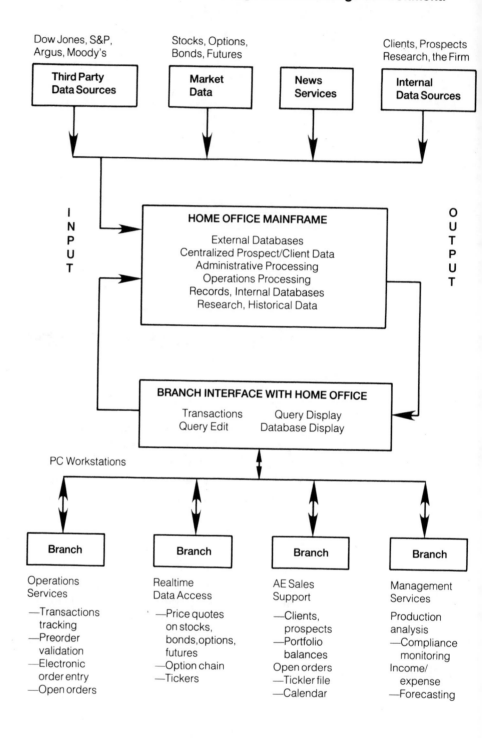

Weekly Reports

- stock record balance report;
- mark to the market report;
- various activity (trading) reports.

Real-time Access to Financial Ticker Services:

- N.Y., American, Boston, Cincinnati, Midwest, Pacific, Philadelphia Stock Exchanges, and NASDAQ and Instinet Montreal, Toronto, Vancouver Stock Exchanges.
- Commodities, Options, Futures—CBOT, CME, IMM, CEC, COMEX, NYMEX, KBOT, MACE, NYFE, OPRA, CBOE, and others.
- London Stock Exchange, London International Financial Futures Exchange, BZW Corporate Information.
- Customized Quotation Display:

    For selected market issues—Last trade, net change, volume/ open interest, bid, ask, day's high/low, and opening/closing ranges.

    Automatic updates, option chains, previous trades, most actives, tickers, market limit indicator, market trends and graphical representations.

    Money markets, bonds, T-bills, foreign exchange, precious metals, energy, automatic worldwide updates.

    Automatic monitoring and alert on selected contracts.

Corporate Databases

- Business description—Interim earnings and dividend, comments, five-year records of earnings/balance sheet, book value, P/E ratio, price range, capitalization primary/secondary SIC codes, address, telephone number.
- News events—earnings (interim), annual reports, history/business, merger/acquisition, management, balance sheets, bankruptcy, contracts, stocks, bonds.

Forecasting and Analytical Tools

- Volume and price charts, overlays, moving averages, crossover of moving averages, on-balance volume, relative strength, volatility factor, trend lines, chart inversion, overlays, data dumps for client analysis.

The following is just an example of how the computer can provide services for brokers, managers, and sales support people. It can provide:

- *Client and prospect profiles*—Name/address, investment objectives, personal interests, special instructions, documents on file, phone numbers, delivery instructions, alternate registration, date of last activity, commissions generated, client 45-day history, location of securities, memos and notes.
- *Portfolio management*—Balances, portfolio valuation, gains/losses (realized/unrealized), dynamic pricing, scratch pad, open orders, dividend and interest dates, offerings and reorganizations.
- *Electronic broker book*—In/out house holdings, tax lots, transaction history.
- *Query*—Open positions, account balances, client specifics.
- *Alerts*—Research, news events, price limits, price movements.
- *Tickler*—Items for attention, morning routine, date events.
- *Management services*—Production analysis, compliance monitoring, income/expense.
- *Operations Service*—Transaction tracking, pre-order validation, electronic order entry, inquiry and update, open orders.
- *Real-time access to financial ticker services.*
- *Databases from industry leaders*—Dow Jones, Standard & Poor's, Argus, Moody's, and others.
- *Communications services.*
- *Office automation*—Word processing, electronic spreadsheet, electronic mail, telemarketing/autodial.

EXERCISE 20:1
Electronic Data Processing

To do this exercise, you must:

- Review the contents of this course
- Check with your operations manager
- List your daily responsibilities
- Observe the branch procedures, ask questions of backoffice staff

List the times during the day when you must work with a computer. Also jot down your duties, for future reference.

- Opening new accounts—

  _____

  _____

- Retrieving and updating client information—

  _____

  _____

- Processing client transactions—

  _____

  _____

- Following the electronic paper trail of a transaction—

  _____

  _____

- Keeping track of credit transactions—

  _____

  _____

- Tickler file for client instructions- -

  _____

  _____

- Accessing real-time securities information—

  _____

  _____

- Accessing news services—

  _____

  _____

- Correspondence and word processing—

  _____

  _____

- Interbranch communication—

  _____

  _____

Glossary*

Accrued interest. The amount of interest owed to the seller by the buyer on transactions involving most bonds and notes.

Added Trade Contract. The last in a series of contract reports (put out by the NSCC) containing the total of previously compared trades from the regular-way contract, supplemental contract sheets, and the trades that were compared through QT, DK, and CHC processing.

ADR. See *American Depository Receipt*.

Agency Transaction. Trade where the firm operates as a broker. The firm executes trades as an agent and charges commission for the service.

All or None. Term used in certain underwritings and also an instruction on an order. All must be completed or the originator of order cannot accept any portion of the order.

American Depository Receipt (ADR). Receipt for shares of stock issued by American banks backed by foreign securities that are on deposit.

AMEX. The American Stock Exchange located at 86 Trinity Place, New York, NY. One of the major stock and option exchanges in the United States.

Amortization. An accounting term meaning apportioning an incurred expense or service over its life.

*A more complete glossary is available: *The Securities Industry Glossary* (New York: New York Institute of Finance, 1986).

Annual Report. Formal presentation of the corporation's financial statements which yearly is sent to its registered stockholders. Any shares registered in a nominee name or in the care of the brokerage firm will require that the firm's proxy department secure copies for those clients and mail them out.

Arbitrage. A process where an industry professional offsets equal positions for an anticipated profit. This concept is usually brought into play when disparities appear in prices of equals.

Asked. The offer side of a quote. A quote is the highest bid and lowest asked (offer) available in the marketplace at a given point in time.

As of. Any trade not processed on the actual trade date will be processed "as of" on that particular day.

Assets. Items owned by the corporation.

Averages. Mathematical computation used to indicate the value of a group of securities. The most popular averages are the *Dow-Jones Industrial Average (DJI), Standard and Poors (S&P) 500,* and the *New York Stock Exchange Composite.* The average may be computed as market-weighted, share-weighted or price-weighted, and it represents an indication of performance.

Balance Sheet. An accounting of the firm's financial condition comprising all assets, liabilities and net worth (ownership). In a balance sheet, *assets = liabilities + net worth.*

BAN. Bond Anticipation Notes. A short-term municipal debt instrument.

Banker Acceptance. Debt instruments used in international trade. They are "discounted" instruments and are part of a group known as money market instruments.

Basis Price. Method of pricing municipal bonds, T-bills, and certain other instruments. Basis price is yield to maturity.

BCC. Boston Clearing Corporation.

Bear. Someone with a perception that the value of the market will fall.

Bearer Form. Refers to securities whose ownership is not recorded. The individual "bearing" the instrument is the assumed owner.

Bear Market. A falling market condition.

Beneficial Instrument. Any instrument in which physical issuance exists in nonregistered form. Bearer of instrument is assumed to be owner.

Beneficial Owner. Term used in security ownership. Securities belonging to customers are most often registered in the name of the brokerage firm or central depository. When this occurs, the actual owner is not recorded on the certificate or on the company books. Therefore, records must be maintained by brokerage firms to determine who the real or beneficial owner is.

Best Efforts Underwriting. An offering of new stock under which the underwriter will do his or her best to place the issue but is not responsible for unsold portions.

Big Board. New York Stock Exchange.

Bid. The buy side of a quote. A quote is comprised of the highest *bid* (price at which someone is willing to buy) and lowest asked (price at which someone is willing to sell).

Blue Chip. Common stocks representing the cream of the corporate world.

Blotter. Another name for a listing. The term is used for operational purposes and usually carries trades and customer account numbers segregated by point of execution.

Blotter Code. A system by which trades are identified by type and place of execution. The structure of the code is necessary to enable the firms to "balance" customer vs. streetside trades.

Blue Sky Rules. Security rules of the various states. A new issued being sold interstate and being more than $1,500,000 in value must be approved for sale in each state. This process is known as blue skying.

Bond. A debt instrument. It is borrowing by a corporation, municipality, federal government, or any other entity. It usually is long-term in nature—10-30 years.

Book Value. A term used in accounting which has no relation to the security's market value. It is usually computed by tracing the value of common shares and adding all balance sheet items appearing below the common stock entry, then dividing by number of common shares.

Box. Another name for vault. It is a place where securities are maintained at the firm.

Break Point Sales. Open-end mutual funds transactions in which the buyer of the fund is acquiring shares at the point where the sales charge reduces to a lower percentage. Break points are quantity levels, established by the fund, at which the percent charge is reduced.

Broker. A multi-meaning term. A broker is an individual who buys or sells securities for his or her customers (stockbroker). Term also refers to a member on an exchange who executes public orders on an agency basis (floor broker or commission house broker). Term is also used for a firm that executes orders for others (brokerage firm).

Broker's Call Rate. The rate that banks charge brokerage firms for the financing of margin accounts and inventory positions.

Brokerage Firm. A partnership or corporation that is in business to provide security services.

BSE. Boston Stock Exchange. Trades equities and is located in Boston, Massachusetts.

Bull. An individual who perceives an upward market.

Bull Market. A term used for a rising market.

Business District Conduct Committee. Part of NASD that investigates and reviews customer complaints or other industry improprieties and renders a verdict.

Buying Power. The margin conversion of "excess." It represents the amount of securities the client can purchase or sell short without having to deposit additional funds.

Call. A call option permits the owner to buy a contracted amount of underlying security at a set price for a predetermined period of time.

Callable. This feature in securities allows issuer to retire the issue when desired. Usually a premium is paid by the issuer should the issue be called.

Capital Gain. An accounting term used for the applicability of tax on trading profit. Trading gains that occur in a year or less are short-term capital gains. Those that cover a period of a year and a day or longer are long-term capital gains. Short-term and long-term capital gains are treated differently for tax purposes.

Capital Loss. An accounting term used for the applicability of tax on a trading loss. Time consideration is the same as for capital gain.

Capitalization. The total amount of common stock, preferred stock, and bonds issued by a corporation.

Capital Stock. Often misused term, it refers to the common and preferred stock of a company.

Cash Account. A customer account in which all securities purchased must be paid for in full by the fifth business day but no later than the seventh business day after trade.

Cash Dividend. Dividends paid to stockholders by corporations from their earnings, paid on a per-share basis.

Cash Sale. Trade that settles on trade date. Used in equities at the end of the year for tax purposes.

CBOE. Chicago Board Option Exchange. Listed option trading was originated by this marketplace on April 26, 1973.

CBT. Chicago Board of Trade. A major commodity exchange located at 141 West Jackson Boulevard, Chicago, Ill.

Certificate. The physical document evidencing ownership (stock certificate) or debt (bond certificate).

Certificates of Deposits. "CDs" are short-term debt instruments issued by banks. Those of larger denominations are negotiable and can be traded in the secondary market.

CFTC. Commodities Future Trading Commission is responsible for the enforcement of rules and regulations of the futures industry.

CHC. Clearing House Comparison is a form used to submit trades to NSCC that have missed normal entry modes. They enter the system on the third business day of a particular trade cycle.

Clearing Corporations. Central receive and distribution center operated for its members, made up of various brokerage firms. Many offer automated systems expedite comparison procedures. Among these are NSCC (National Securities Clearing Corporation) and OCC (Options Clearing Corporation).

Closed-End Fund. Once the initial offering has been completed, the fund stops offering and acquiring its shares. The value of the fund is now determined by supply and demand rather than net asset value.

CME. Chicago Mercantile Exchange. A major commodity exchange located in Chicago, Illinois.

Collateral. Value being pledged to support a loan.

Collateral Trust Bond. Debt instruments issued by corporations and backed by securities of a different corporation.

COMEX. Commodity Exchange located at 4 World Trade Center, New York, New York.

Combination Order. A combination order is used in listed option trading. It is the simultaneous entry to buy or sell a put and a call having the same underlying but different series designations.

Commercial Paper. A short-term debt issued by corporations. Its rate of interest is set at issuance and can be realized only if held to maturity.

Commission. (1) Amount charged by a firm on an agency transaction. (2) The method by which account executives are compensated.

Commission House Broker. A type of floor broker who is employed by a brokerage house to execute orders on the floor of an exchange for the firm and its customers.

Common Stock. Issued in shares, represents ownership of a corporation. These stockholders have the privilege to vote for the management and receive dividends after all other obligations of the corporation have been satisfied.

Comparison. Process by which two sides of a trade (brokerage firms) agree to the terms of a transaction. Comparison can be either through a clearing corporation or on a trade-for-trade basis (without the clearing corporation).

Confirmation. Trade invoices issued to customers of the brokerage firms. It is written notice of the trade, giving price, security description, settlement money, trade, and settlement date plus other pertinent information.

Continuous Net Settlement. The process by which previous day's fail positions are included in the next day's settling position.

Convertible Issue or Convertible Bond. Convertible feature permits the issue holder to convert into another issue, usually common stock. It is a privilege that is contained in some issues and can be used once. The preferred or bond holder can convert from one issue to another but not back.

Cooling-Off Period. Period from time the registration statement on a new issue is filed with the SEC until the effective date of the offering. The period is usually 20 days in duration.

Corporate Bond. Debt instruments issued by a corporation. They are usually fixed income. That is, they carry a fixed rate of interest. From issuance, the life of a bond may be as long as 30 years.

Credit Balance. The client's fund balance in a cash or margin account.

Cumulative Preferred. All dividends owed to the preferred stock owner, which were not paid when due, accumulate and must be paid (including present dividends) before common stock may receive any dividend.

Curb Exchange. An old and archaic name for the American Stock Exchange (AMEX).

CUSIP. Committee on Uniform Security Identification Procedure is an intraindustry security coding service. Each security has its own unique number.

DBO. Delivery Balance Order issued by the Clearing Corp. to firms that, after netting that day's trades, have a delivery or sale position remaining. It defines what is to be delivered to whom.

DK. "Don't Know" is used throughout the industry as a term meaning "unknown item." The term is used on the AMEX for equity transactions that cannot be compared by the morning of T+3 (trade plus three business days). It is also used over-the-counter for comparison purposes.

DTC. Depository Trust Company.

Dated Date. The first day that interest starts to accrue on newly issued bonds.

Day Order. An order that, if not executed on the day it is entered, expires at the close of that day's trading.

Day Trade. Buying and selling of the same security on the same day. This type of transaction has certain margin implications.

Dealer. A firm that functions as a market maker and as such, positions the security to buy and sell versus the public or brokerage community.

Debenture. A form of bond secured by nothing but the good name and reputation of the issuing corporation.

Debit Balance. The amount of loan in a margin account.

Deed of Trust. The term under which a corporate bond is issued. It appears on the *face of the certificate*. The *indenture*.

Depository. A central location for securities.

Depository Trust Company. Also known as DTC, it is a central depository for equity and debt securities. It has as its customers brokerage firms and banks.

Depreciation. An accounting term used to write off the value of machinery and equipment against earnings over the life of the equipment.

Differential. The fraction of a point added to the price of buy odd lot orders or subtracted from the price of sell odd lot orders. The charge represents compensation to the specialists for executing an odd lot order.

Director. A member of a corporate board elected by the stockholders.

Discretionary Account. A type of client account requiring special permission of the firm's management. The account executive is permitted to buy and sell securities for the client *without* the client's prior permission on each trade.

Discretionary Order. An order entered by the account executive for a discretionary account. The account executive decides on security, quantity, and price to be traded.

Distribution. The process by which a large block of stock is sold to many investors.

Dividend. Paid on *shares* only. Preferred stock carries dividend amount in description. Common stock pays when declared.

Dollar Cost Averaging. A method used in mutual funds by which the clients invest the same dollar amount periodically. As mutual funds permit the buying of fractional shares, all the investors' payments are used in the acquisition of fund shares.

DOT. Designated Order Turnaround is an order routing and execution reporting system of the NYSE. Orders up to 599 shares may be entered by member firms through this system.

Double Taxation. Dividends are paid from after-tax earnings of a corporation. They are taxed again as ordinary income to the stockholder.

Downstairs Trader. Operates on the floor of an exchange and "trades" his positions against the public market.

Down Tick. A listed equity trade below the last different sale.

DNI. Do Not Increase is an instruction placed on buy limit, sell stop, and stop limit GTC orders, that informs order-handling personnel not to increase the share quantity of the order in the payment of a stock dividend.

DNR. Do Not Reduce is an instruction placed on buy limit, sell stop, and stop limit GTC orders that informs order-handling personnel not to reduce the price of the order by the amount of dividends if and when paid by the corporation.

Due Bills. IOUs that are primarily used in settlement of trades involved in dividend and split situations when the shares to be received are as yet unavailable for delivery.

Due Diligence Meeting. The last meeting between corporate officials and underwriters prior to the issuance of the security. At the meeting, the facts contained in the prospectus are discussed.

Earnings Report. A corporate financial statement that reports all earnings and expenses netting to a profit or loss and therefore is sometimes referred to as the P&L (profit and loss) statement.

Effective Date. The first date after the cooling-off period of a new issue when the security can be offered.

Equipment Trust Bonds. Debt instruments issued by some corporations backed by "rolling stock." (Airline companies could issue bonds backed by their planes, railroad companies on the locomotives and freight cars, and so on.)

Equity in Account. The portion of a customer account that reflects the customer's ownership interest.

Escrow Receipts. Guarantees of delivery issued by qualified banks to clearing corporations, such as OCC, on behalf of the bank's customer. The member firm acts as a conduit for these documents.

Ex-Dividend Date. The first day on which the purchaser of the security would not be entitled to the dividend. It is also the day that price of the security drops to the next highest fraction of the dividend amount.

Expiration Month. Month in which an option will cease to exist (expires).

Face Value. The amount of debt appearing on the face of certificates which the issuer is responsible for paying at maturity.

Factor Table. Tables used to compute the current principal outstanding on Ginnie Maes and Freddie Macs.

Fails. Transactions that are not settled on the appropriate day.

Fail to Deliver. An open commitment by a selling firm to deliver a contracted issue if the parties to the trade were unable to settle on the settlement date.

Fail to Receive. An open commitment by a purchasing firm to receive the security that was not settled on settlement date.

FAST. An acronym for Fast Automatic Stock Transfer, a service offered by DTC.

Fed Funds. Term used for same-day money transfers between the banks by use of the Fed wire, drawing down and lending reserve deposits by a member bank of the Federal Reserve.

Figuration. That part of the P&S function responsible for the computation of trades.

Fill or Kill (FOK). An order that requires total execution of the entire quantity immediately. If this cannot be accomplished, the order is cancelled.

Fiscal Year. An accounting term. Businesses maintain their financial records on an annual basis. This cycle does not have to coincide with the calendar year, and therefore it is known as the fiscal year.

Flat. Bond trading without accrued interest.

Floor Broker. A member of an exchange "owns a seat" and by being a member is permitted to conduct business on that exchange floor.

Free Stock. Loanable securities that are comprised of firm-owned securities and securities in margin accounts. These securities can be used for loan or hypothecation.

Futures. A long-term contract on an underlying instrument, usually a grain, precious metal, or interest rate instrument, by which the buyer and seller lock in a price for a later delivery.

GNMA. Government National Mortgage Association guarantees prompt payment for interest and principal on mortgages.

GNMA Modified Pass-Through Securities. Instruments comprised of a pool of mortgages that have been guaranteed by FHA or insured by FMHA and VA, GNMAs pay interest and principal on a monthly basis.

Government. Pertains to issues of the federal government.

GO. General obligation. Refers to a muni bond where the ability to pay back principal and interest is based on the full taxing power of the issuing municipality.

Growth Stock. Stock of a company in a new industry or an emerging industry.

GTC. A good-til-cancelled or open order is a type of order that does not expire at the end of the day it is entered and remains in force until it is either executed or cancelled.

Hypothecation. Process by which firms pledge margin securities at a bank to secure the funds necessary to carry debit balances.

ID Revenue. ID revs, industrial revs, or industrial revenue bonds are a form of muni bond whose ability to pay interest and principal is based on revenue earned from an industrial complex.

Immediate or Cancel (IOC). Instruction on an order that requires as many lots as can be filled immediately and the rest cancelled.

Income Bonds. These are issued when the ability of the issuing company to pay interest is questioned. They are speculative financial products because they will pay a high rate of interest only when it is earned.

Indenture. Explains the terms under which a corporate bond has been issued. (deed of trust).

Issue. A security.

Legal Transfer. Involves transferring the registration of certain issues involving corporate name, security registered in the name of deceased, certain type of trust, etc. These types of transfers require legal documentation in addition to normal forms.

Liabilities. An accounting term. All claims against the corporation are known as liabilities. Included in this group are accounts payable, salaries payable, and bonds.

Limit Orders. Sets the highest price buyer is willing to pay or lowest price seller is willing to accept. Buy orders may be executed at or below limit price but never higher. Sell orders may be executed at or above the limit price.

Limited Tax Bonds. Muni bonds whose ability to pay back principal and interest is based on a restricted ability to tax.

Liquidation. (1) The closing out of a position is referred to as liquidation. (2) An action taken by the margin department when a client hasn't paid for a purchase.

Liquidity. A key factor in our industry—that is, the ability to buy and sell securities easily.

Listed Stock. The stock of a company that has qualified for trading on an exchange.

Load. Sales charge associated with some open-end mutual funds. The amount of the sales charge on purchases of the fund shares from the fund determines the load.

Loan Value. The amount of money or percentage of market value that the customer may borrow from the firm on transactions in a margin account.

Long Position. Securities in a customer account.

Management Company. The group of individuals responsible for the managing of a mutual fund's portfolio.

Margin Department. Responsible for ensuring that customer's accounts are being maintained in accordance with various rules and regulations.

Margin Account. Permits the firm to lend the customer money on purchases of securities on short sales.

Mark-to-Market. Process by which security position values are brought up to their current value. This includes securities and commodities in margin accounts, trading inventory, etc.

Market Maker. Another term for dealer or specialist. Market makers stand ready to trade against the public and therefore to make a market in particular issues.

Market Order. Accepts current market price. Buy market orders accept current offer. Sell market orders accept current bid.

Mark-Up. The amount of the charge being imposed on principal transactions.

Maturity. The end of a loan period when bonds and other debt instruments must be repaid.

Mark Down. The charge being subtracted from the price on a sell principal transaction.

MCC—Midwest Clearing Corporation. Clearing corporation of the Midwest Stock Exchange.

Member Firm. Partnership or corporation that owns a membership on an exchange.

Member. Name used for an individual who owns a membership on an exchange.

Merger. Occurs when two or more companies consolidate into one through the exchange of stock.

Minimum Maintenance. The amount to which the equity in a margin account may fall before the client must deposit additional equity.

Money Market Fund. A form of mutual fund that specializes in securities of the money market, such as T bills and commercial paper.

Money Market Instruments. Short-term debt instruments that reflect current interest rates and, because of their short life, do not respond to interest rate changes as longer-term instruments do. Examples of money market instruments are U.S. treasury bills, commercial paper, and bankers acceptances.

Mortgage Bond. Debt instrument issued by corporations that is secured by real estate (factories, office buildings, etc.) owned by the corporation.

MSRB. Municipal Securities Rule-Making Board establishes rules and regulations to be followed in the trading, dealings, and customer relationships concerned in municipal securities.

Muni. Slang for municipal debt instrument—issues of state or local governments.

Municipal Bond. Long-term debt instrument issued by state or local governments. It usually carries a fixed rate of interest, paid semiannually.

Muni Notes. Short-term debt of state or local government. Most popular are RANs, BANs, and TANs.

Mutual Fund. A pooling of money for specific investment purposes. The fund is managed by a management company that is responsible for adhering to the purpose of the fund.

NASD. National Association of Securities Dealers is an industry "self"-regulating authority (SRO). Its jurisdiction includes the over-the-counter market.

NASDAQ. National Association of Securities Dealers Automated Quotation Service is a communication network used to broadcast the quotation for qualified over-the-counter securities.

Negotiable. A legal term referring to the ability to transfer ownership or title. A non-negotiable instrument should not be paid for because it has no value.

Net Asset Value. The bid side of an open-end fund quote. The offer side includes the sales charge. The net asset value is the value of the fund divided by the number of outstanding fund shares.

Net-by-Net. Original form of merging fail positions into settling trades. This process greatly reduced the number of fails open on firms' books. It originated at the Pacific Clearing Corp. (PCC).

1933 Act. *See* Truth in Security Act.

1934 Act. *See* Securities and Exchange Act.

No-Load. Refers to an open-end fund that does not impose a sales charge on customers who buy their shares.

Not Held (NH). An instruction on an order that informs the broker or trader that executions are not dependent on time; the executor should take whatever time is necessary to insure good executions.

NSCC. National Securities Clearing Corp. is a major clearing corporation offering many services to the brokerage community. This includes comparison of NYSE, AMEX, and over-the-counter transactions.

NYFE. New York Futures Exchange is a commodity market located at 30 Broad Street, New York, New York, specialized in index futures.

NYSE. New York Stock Exchange is located at 11 Wall Street, New York, New York. It is a primary market for buying and selling securities of major corporations.

OBO. Order Book Official is an employee of certain exchanges who executes limit order on behalf of the membership.

Odd Lot. Trade whose quantity is smaller than the standard unit of trading (often less than 100 shares).

Offer. The offer side of a quote. A quote represents the highest bid and lowest asked (offer) available in the market place at a given point in time.

Open-End Fund. Mutual fund that makes a continuous offering of its shares and stands ready to buy its shares upon surrender by the shareholders. The share value is determined by net asset value of the fund.

Option. Contracts between the buyer and seller of the option that permit the holder to buy (call) or sell (put) a predetermined quantity of a defined issue for a specific period of time at a preestablished price.

OCC—Option Clearing Corporation. The central or main clearing corporation for listed options. At the present time, options traded on any SEC-regulated exchange can be settled through OCC, thereby expediting closeouts and the like.

Repo's. Repurchase agreements used to finance certain government and money market inventory positions.

Revenue Bonds. A form of muni bonds where the ability to pay interest and principal is based on revenue earned from a project.

Rights (Preemptive rights). May be part of corporation's charter and/or by-laws. Additional shares of issued security *must* be offered to current owners in proportion to their holding before it can be offered to others. Usually one right is issued for each outstanding share.

Risk Arbitrage. Performed by a professional trader who takes on a position in anticipation of an event occurring (e.g., merger, takeover). If the event happens, the arbitrageur could profit; if it doesn't, a substantial loss could result.

ROTN. Rejected Option Trade Notice is a procedure (and form) by which an uncompared listed option trade is returned for reconcilement to broker who executed it.

Round Lot. A trading unit. Common stocks trade in 100-share "round lots." A round lot in bonds traded over the counter is 5 bonds.

Rules of Fair Practice. Part of the NASD rules that govern the dealings of firms with the public.

SCCP. Stock Clearing Corporation of Philadelphia is the clearing corporation for PHLX.

SEC. Securities and Exchange Commission is the federal agency responsible for law enforcement of the securities industry.

Secondary Market. The after-market. The initial offering of a security is the primary offering. It can later be sold, then resold in the secondary market. The over-the-counter market is the largest secondary market, issue-wise.

Securities and Exchange Act. This Act, also known as the 1934 Act, governs the lending of money by brokerage firms (Reg T), including short-sale (uptick) rule and insider or controlled person requirements.

Segregation. Term used for securities that must be "locked up" by the firm. It represents fully paid-for securities or that portion of a margin account in excess of loanable securities. The firm may not use these securities for hypothication or loan.

Selling Against the Box. A short sale entered into where the client is also long the security. It is used to "box" a profit or loss for application in another period of time.

Serial. Serial bonds are an issue of bonds that mature over a given period of years.

Settled Inventory. That portion of a trader's position which the firm has paid for and maintains. It is this portion that must be financed.

Settlement Date. The day when a transaction is to be completed. The buyer is to pay and the seller is to deliver on this day.

Settlement Date Inventory. Refers to the security positions on settlement date. It includes vault, transfer, fails, and so on.

Short Account. Account in which the customer has sold security not owned or does not intend to deliver against sale. Before customer can sell short, margin account must be opened.

Short Exempt. A short sale that is exempt from the short sale rules is said to be short exempt. For example, the buying of a convertible preferred, submitting conversion instructions, and selling the common stock short before the stock is received would be short exempt.

Short Position. A position in a customer's account in which the customer owes the firm securities.

Short Sale. The selling of securities not owned or not intended to be delivered. The short seller "borrows" the stock to make delivery with the intent to buy it back at a later date at a lower price.

Size. Term used to describe the number of shares available. For example, the quote and size on a stock is 9¼-½ 3 × 5. This translates: the bid is 9¼, the offer 9½, 300 shares are bid, 500 shares are offered.

SIAC. Securities Industry Automated Corporation is the computer facility and trade processing company for NYSE, AMEX, NSCC, and PCC.

Specialist. A member of certain SEC regulated exchanges that *must* make a market in assigned securities. The specialist also acts as a broker in executing orders entrusted to him/her.

Speculator. A client willing to assume high risk.

Spread. (1) A long and short option position in either puts or calls on the same underlying stock but different series. (2) The difference between the bid and offer sides of a quote. (3) In underwriting, the difference between what the issuer receives from the underwriter and what the security is sold for to the public.

Stock Ahead. A term used when other orders have priority.

Stock Dividends. Paid by corporations from retained earnings. The corporation declares the dividend as a percentage of shares outstanding.

Stock/Bond Power. A form used as a substitute for endorsement of a certificate. When completed, the form can be attached to the certificate(s) and processed for delivery or transfer.

Stockholder of Record. A term used to explain who is entitled to receive the dividend. A client must be owner of the security on the night the company closes its books for registration.

Stock Loan/Borrow. This department is part of the cashiering function responsible for lending excess seg stock and obtaining stock when needed by the firm.

Stock Record. A ledger on which all security movements and positions are recorded. The record is usually in two formats: one showing the previous day's security movements, the other the current security positions for which the firm is responsible.

Stock Splits. A restructuring of outstanding shares without any direct benefit to the shareholders. Split-ups increase the number of shares and are offset by a reduction in the share's market value. Split-downs reduce the shares outstanding and are offset by a rise in the share's market value.

Stop Order. A memorandum stop that becomes a market order when the price is reached or passed. Buy stops are entered above the current market price, sell stops are entered below.

Stop Limit Order. A memorandum order that becomes a limit, instead of a market order, at or through the indicated price. Buy stop limit orders are entered above the current market; sell stops extend below.

Stock. Represents ownership of corporations issued in "shares."

Straddle. Long or short positions of puts and calls having the same underlying security and same series designation.

Street Name. Refers to securities which are registered in the name of a brokerage firm or bank and is acceptable as good delivery. Included in this group are securities registered in the name of depositories.

Street Side. A terminology used to describe the opposing firms' side of trades. (For example, customer agency transactions consummated on an exchange must be offset and balanced against the "opposing firm.")

Strike Price. The price at which an option can be exercised. For example, the owner of A Call Zap April *40* can call in (buy) 100 shares of ABC *at $40* per share. (Exercise Price.)

Syndicate. The name of the group formed to perform an underwriting. Includes underwriting manager(s) and other underwriters.

Take-Over. Take-over of a corporation occurs when an alien group acquires the power to "control" a company, thereby ousting the current management. The take-over can occur via a proxy fight or acquisition of a sufficient quantity of common stock.

TAN. Tax Anticipation Notes are a form of short-term muni debt.

Tape. A broadcasting facility that disseminates listed trades in order of their occurrences.

Tax-Exempt Bonds. Municipal securities whose interest is free from federal income tax.

Tender Offer. The offer made by one company or individuals for shares of another company. The offer may be in cash or security form.

Trade Date. The actual day the trade occurred.

Trade Date Inventory. A term used by trading departments. It refers to the position of their inventory at the start of the trading day.

Trade-for-Trade Settlement. The form in which original buying clearing firm settles a trade with the original selling firm. It is excluded from a clearing corporation's netted comparison systems.

Transfer. The process by which securities are re-registered to new owners. The old securities are cancelled and new ones issued to the new registrants.

Transfer Agent. A commercial bank that retains the name and address of owners of registered securities. They are also responsible for re-registering securities to the name of new owners.

Truth in Security Act. 1933 Act, the federal regulation governing the issuance of new corporate securities.

$2 Broker. Term used for a member of an exchange who executes orders for other member firms and charges a fee for each execution.

Underlying. The security or commodity behind an option or futures contract.

Underwriter. The commercial banker or brokerage firm that acts as a conduit by taking the new issues from the issuer (corporation or municipality) and reselling it to the public (Investment Banker).

Underwriting. The process by which investment bankers bring new issues to the market.

Underwriting Manager. Investment banker whose client is the corporation wanting to bring out a new issue (negotiated) or lead firm in a group that is competing with other group(s) for a new issue (competitive).

Uniform Practice Code. Part of the NASD rules that govern the dealing of firms with each other.

Unit Trust. The grouping of certain types of securities in "packages" deposited with a trustee (e.g., muni bonds, corporate bonds). The ownership of the package is divided into parts (units), and the individual parts (units) are then sold in the marketplace.

U.S. Treasury Bills (T bills). Shortest-term instrument of the federal government. Discounted in form, issue doesn't exceed one year at issuance. Three-month (90-day) or six-month (180-day) paper is very common.

U.S. Treasury Bonds. Longest-term debt of the Fed, issued in coupon form for periods of 10 to 30 years.

U.S. Treasury Notes. Intermediate debt of the federal government. Usually issued for 1 to 10 years.

Unsecured Debit. Occurs when the market value in the account (securities) is less than the debit balance. Liquidation of the position would leave the account with a debit balance and no means to cover the loan. Therefore, the loans are unsecured.

Upstairs Trader. Operates from a trading desk located in the firm. Traders on the floor of the exchanges are known as "downstairs traders."

Uptick. A listed equity trade which is higher than the last different sale.

Warrants. Issued by corporations, usually with another issue of security (such as one warrant + one bond = one unit). Warrant allows owner to purchase the corporation's stock for a certain price over the life of the warrant (as long as 10 or 20 years).

When Issued. Applies to securities that are about to be issued but settlement date is not set. Usually common stock issued under a rights offering will trade "WI." Also, government bills auctioned on Tuesday but settled on Thursday will trade in this manner.

Wire House. A firm that maintains a branch network that communicates via teletype.

Yield. A rate of return on investments. Many computations give different yields, such as current yield and yield to maturity.

Zero Coupon Bond. Bonds that do not pay interest but instead are discounted. At maturity, bonds will pay full face value.

INDEX